# BEYOND
# HONOR

A Promise Kept

# BEYOND HONOR

JAMES BUTLER

TATE PUBLISHING
AND ENTERPRISES, LLC

Published by Tate Publishing & Enterprises, LLC
127 E. Trade Center Terrace | Mustang, Oklahoma 73064 USA
1.888.361.9473 | www.tatepublishing.com

Tate Publishing is committed to excellence in the publishing industry. The company reflects the philosophy established by the founders, based on Psalm 68:11,
*"The Lord gave the word and great was the company of those who published it."*

Book design copyright © 2013 by Tate Publishing, LLC. All rights reserved.
*Cover design by Joel Uber*
*Interior design by Jomel Pepito*

Published in the United States of America

ISBN: 978-1-62563-268-5
1. Family & Relationships / General
2. Biography & Autobiography / Military
13.03.20

# Dedication

This book is dedicated to my son, Sergeant Jacob Lee Butler, my wife, Cindy, and to Jake's brothers James C. Butler Jr., Josh M. Butler, Joe D. Butler, and Justin M. Butler. And to all that believed in giving whatever it takes to keep our freedom. This book could never have been written without the help and support of the people that stood beside me after Jake's death and all that stood beside Jake before and during April 1, 2003. Thanks to Jake's grandparents, Robert and Nancy Butler, and also to all of Jake's aunts, uncles, cousins, and friends. Thank you to the military for their support and the United States government for how they strive to protect the rights and freedom for everyone.

# Table of Contents

# Acknowledgments

A special thanks to Jake's platoon that he was with on April 1, 2003. I know this will be a day that will be on their minds until the end of time. I know they did all they could on the day Jake died. It was not only the end of Jake's life as we knew it here on earth, but it was a new beginning for him. As time goes on, we will all get a chance for a new beginning.

I would also like to thank Chrissy, Jake's sister-in-law, for all she did for Cindy and me through the ups and downs in 2003. Also, a special thanks goes to the little people back then in my life: Shelby, KK, and Jess. I love you, and may God bless each and every one of you.

I would also like to say thanks to Colonel Snow, who always believed in me and in what a father has to do for his family. Colonel Snow, you made my mission for Jake happen; you helped me complete my promise. Thank you.

I would also like to thank all the people who helped with all the pictures to make this book happen. Thank you to Jamie Gibson, Doreen and Kerry Frazier, Joe Butler, Paul Turner, and Sara Elmer for helping me get this book to where it is today. Last and certainly not least, I would like to thank Ty and Bobbie Butler for believing in me and helping me get the book into production.

This book is from me as a tribute to my son Jake who will *never be forgotten*.

"Until we meet again, Jake. "Love you forever."

Dad

# Introduction

As a parent you can only protect and guide your children into adulthood. When they reach adulthood and move on and out all you can do as a parent is pray for them and help them in any way. However on April 1, 2003 we were not prepared for the knock on the door to tell us that our son, SGT Jacob Lee Butler, was killed in Iraq. And so my journey began.

# In the Beginning

When I met my wife, Cindy, there was something there that was real and meaningful. I felt that we were meant to be together. We were young and crazy, but we knew we were *in love*. Our love was never about money. We never had much, but we were content with what we had. It wasn't about appearances either; those things didn't matter to us. What mattered was what was beneath the surface. The feelings we had for one another were deep inside; they came from the heart. No one knew what we were feeling except ourselves. It's something you can't really explain and put into words. As time went on, our love grew stronger for one another.

We started dating shortly after we met in the spring of 1974. I remember our first date so well. We went to see the Beach Boys in concert. It was a fun experience, and I also learned that Cindy had a unique way of driving. She would always take off her shoes, put her left foot up on the dash, and use her right foot to drive. I always made comments about her "short little feet" because I thought they were pretty darn adorable! My little sister tagged along that night too. It definitely wasn't as fun as it could've been without her!

As time went on, we started talking about getting married and starting a family. It was our dream to be blessed with six children. We agreed that Cindy would be a stay-at-home mom, and I would work. I knew my part wasn't going to be easy, but neither was hers. We were young and didn't know what it took to raise a family. We agreed that we would work together as much as possible, as every mother and father should. We knew that each child would have their own unique problems growing up and that we would always help them as much as we could. We knew we could always ask for help from our parents if we got overwhelmed because they had always been there to support us in every part of our lives.

Cindy and I were married on April 19, 1975. We were already *well* on our way with starting a family because shortly before our wedding, Cindy found out she was pregnant with our first child, James. He arrived seven short months later on October 14, 1975. Joshua, our second child, was born on January 24, 1977. I was in the hospital when Cindy told me she was pregnant with him. I had just survived a nightmare; my lung collapsed earlier that day while I was swimming. I could feel the love and the joy slowly push away the pain and the fear; it was like the sun just rose in my soul.

In 1978, we were surprised with twins! My wife and I realized there was something different about this pregnancy. The first difference: she had gained more weight during this pregnancy than she did in the last two pregnancies. The second difference: she grew to the point where I had to help her out of bed every morning before I left for work. That's when our doctor decided to take a light x-ray, finding *two* babies instead of one. Those two, Joe and Jake, arrived two weeks later on April 26, 1978. Joe was first, and Jake came less than four minutes later.

Less than a year later, Cindy was already pregnant with her fifth. This time, I was really hoping Cindy would get her girl. Toward the end of her pregnancy, she could tell there was something wrong. This baby didn't kick like all of the other babies did. On July 3, 1979, Justin was born with spina bifida. Early on, he had a lot of medical problems, but they have slowly gotten better over time.

As I saw each and every new life come into this world, it brought joy and happiness to my wife and me. It was as if our love had grown into a beautiful red rose. Soon, we had our big family. Cindy still wanted a little girl, but we decided not to have any more since five kids already demanded enough of our attention.

I knew it was hard keeping up with all of us, but Cindy did everything with ease and turned out to be an amazing mother and wife. She made sure they ate three meals a day every day and made sure they did their homework every day after school. She helped each of them with their homework and school projects and took care of them when they were sick. They always had clean clothes to wear and a happy home to live in.

After our last son was born, I remember someone asking me why we had all of our children at such a young age. I explained that I wanted to grow old with them. You see, time goes by faster than you think. As a family, we have stuck together through good times and bad. Cindy lost her dad in the fall of 1992, and her mom passed away a few years later in 1995. I couldn't imagine what she was going through because I had never lost a parent. I knew it had to be hard for her, but our love for each other, along with the love from our boys, helped get her through it. I am lucky to still have both of my parents, and I count my blessings for it.

When the boys were between the ages of five and nine years old, they (along with my wife) decided they wanted a dog. So they (I should say "we") started looking for one. Cindy found a tiny toy poodle in the paper and asked if we could look at it. We all loaded up in the car and went to look at the puppy. When we got to the breeder's house, there were several other little puppies in the litter. The boys went around and looked at each puppy with a critical eye and finally chose the one they wanted. They picked a black male that was seven weeks old, and we paid one hundred dollars for him. At the time, we thought that was too much money to be spending on something we didn't really need. But it ended up making the boys *so* happy that it turned out to be a really good investment. As we watched the boys play with their new puppy, Cindy told them that it needed a name. After a few quiet minutes, she mentioned that the puppy looked like a *Mister*. So Mister it was!

As Mister grew older, he would wait at the front door every day after school to watch for the bus to arrive. When he saw the boys get off the bus and start to walk down the driveway, he would jump on the door in anticipation in order to get our attention to let him out. The boys would always greet Mister with excitement and would play with him until it was time to do their homework.

After a couple of years, Cindy thought it was time for Mister to have a misses. I knew she wouldn't take no for an answer, so we went out and found a two-year-old female poodle. We bred the two of them together, and nine weeks later, she had a litter of puppies! The boys were so excited because they got to watch her have the puppies. They thought it was the greatest thing they had ever seen. However, after a year and a half of repeated attempts to potty train Misses, we decided it was time to let her go. She had originally been housebroken, but after she had had puppies, she reverted back to being a puppy herself. We found a good home for her that was able to patiently work with her on her issues.

As the boys grew up, I watched them work hard in the real world in order to survive, and I have seen them become more successful. Each of them continuously strives to make their lives better every day. I hope and pray they will not forget where they came from and that they are not any better than the next person. Cindy and I raised them with structure and discipline as well as love, compassion, and understanding. I hope they will never forget that and use our example to raise their children. I am *very* proud of the men they have become today.

# Our First Home

The first house Cindy and I bought was a little white house with a black roof. It had yellow flowers all across the front and trees surrounding it. The house was comfortable, but it was only about seven hundred square feet; it was small, but it was a *home*. We learned that it used to be a two-car garage before it was converted into a house. It had two bedrooms, one bathroom, a kitchen, and a living room. As our family grew, it became too small for the seven of us. Cindy and I knew we were done having children, so our family was complete. All the boys would stay in one room for the time being until we were able to add more space. We were able to make the best of what we had. We put two bunk beds and a single twin in one room for the boys. It was tight, but it worked. After living this way for a little over a year, we decided to add a great room to the house.

One day I started to draw up plans for our room addition. When I got done with the plans, the house had gone from a meager seven hundred square feet to over 1,500 square feet! Now it was time to start working. The boys were small and young, and they did as much as they could. I received help from my mom, dad, Cindy, my brothers, and my friends. During this time, the boys learned one of the greatest values of work: working together as a team. What we had to do to the old house wasn't easy; we built the new house over the old house and tore the old house down while we were living in it.

After we finished the house, we took a step back to see what we had accomplished. It made me feel good to see what hard work and ambition produced. The boys loved it because they had more room to run and play. It took us eight months from start to finish, and we stuck together throughout the whole process. In the end, the finished product was *amazing*! As time goes by, the boys, Cindy, and I drive by the old house on Farley Street to reminisce on days past.

# In the Past with Jake

In 1984, I had a job of driving a dump truck. One day I was running some loads of sand, and the truck broke down, preventing me from being able to unload it. I brought the truck home to fix it, along with the twenty-two tons of sand I was hauling. I couldn't fix the truck with all the sand in it, so I had to dump all the sand in the driveway. Even though it was hard work, I got a smile out of it because the boys had a blast playing in all the sand. Jake had some soldier action figures he played with, and when July 4 had come around, the boys decided to blow them up with firecrackers. Right then, seeing the interest in Jake's eyes, I knew he was headed for the military.

As Jake was growing up, he was always trying to make a buck on something he found; he was a survivor. Whatever it was, it generally needed to be fixed up. He would always fix it and then sell it. He would always get what he invested in it, plus a little more.

When Jake and Joe were thirteen, they worked for a local farmer named Roger. At the farm, they put up hay and helped milk and feed the cows. When they turned fourteen, they began to drive the tractors. They learned how to cut and rake hay as well as disk and plant crops. Once they learned this, they wanted to learn more and do something different. So they went to work in a greenhouse.

The boys loved working in the greenhouse. It was hard and dirty work, but they seemed to enjoy it. They liked to watch the seeds grow into beautiful plants. On Mother's Day that year, each boy brought a plant home to their mother. They brought a great deal of happiness to their mother; she always loved the flowers the boys gave her. This was one of the ways the boys showed her how much they loved her.

When Jake turned sixteen, he wanted to have a regular job that paid a little more money. He found a job at a grocery store in Wellsville, Kansas; he started as a stocker and sacker. The store's owner, Dwayne, seemed to be happy to have Jake. After about a year, Dwayne and Jake built a trusting relationship with one another. Dwayne asked Jake if he would be interested in being a part-time manager. I remember Jake asking for my advice; I told him it would be a good step forward, but there would be a lot more responsibility. He looked at me and agreed and took the job. He closed the store at nights and opened it on the weekends. It meant a little more money, but more importantly, it gave Jake more independence. As time went on, Jake wanted more responsibility. It wasn't that he wasn't satisfied with the work at the store, but he wanted to make a difference in the world.

In the spring of 1994, my family and I decided to open a bait-and-tackle shop. We called it Butler Bait and Tackle. The boys thought it was neat to see the excitement on the customers' faces when they brought in all the different fish they had caught. We had a special service for our customers: if they brought in the fish they caught, we would take a picture of them with their fish. Jake especially liked the bait shop. If he ever needed any tackle for one of his late-night fishing trips, all he would have to do was walk down the driveway. The bait shop lasted for a little over two years, and then we began having problems with the zoning. We ended up having to close it down. It was a sad time for the whole family, especially the boys.

As the summer started to arrive in 1995, the boys would get together and start getting ready for demolition derby season. They went out looking for old junk cars they could put together to run in the derby. They brought their cars back to the house, took out the entire interior, pulled the windows out, braced the driver's door, and did whatever it took to get the car running. James and Josh were the ones that would drive. Jake, Joe, and Justin did a lot of the tearing apart and putting back together.

For some reason, I was conned into driving one year. It was a lot of fun, but I was sore the next day from being bumped and banged around so much. I remember one of the cars they brought back was from a farmer who was a good friend of the family, Floyd Minot. As we began to work on the car, we used a five-gallon can with gas in it and a hose that went from the can to the carburetor to get the car running. As I poured gas into the carburetor, it backfired, catching the cup I was using to pour fuel into the carburetor on fire. As the flames started to engulf the engine compartment, I dropped the cup next to the gas can, and everyone took off running, yelling, "Shoot!" I looked over at the boys and their friends laughing at me. I had to laugh myself. I reached over, grabbed the fire extinguisher, and put the fire out. The whole time the boys stood their laughing. It doesn't matter if you're young or old; we all make dumb mistakes. We got lucky that time, and it was a good thing no one got hurt.

One Saturday night around 12:30 a.m., I received a call from James, my oldest son, who asked me if I could come and tow his truck back home. I asked him what was wrong with it, and he told me that he had blown out the transfer-case. This is the part of the transmission that locks the vehicle in four-wheel drive. Jake was at home that night, so I asked him if he could go with me to help get James's truck home. He looked at me and laughed and said, "Sure." We took Jake's Blazer, which had four-wheel drive, and headed toward Baldwin, Kansas. On the way, Jake and I started talking. I remember listening to Jake talking; I thought it was pretty neat that if one of the boys had a problem, the others would help them out.

We found James after driving up and down the dirt roads for a while. We were able to get to where his truck was, but he was stuck in twelve to eighteen inches of mud. The boys volunteered to lie in the mud to hook up the chains. We started to drag James's truck because it wouldn't roll. It seemed like we were just crawling along at a snail's pace. It took us two hours to drag his truck for one mile. We got his truck to my brother's house around 5:00 a.m. and headed to work an hour later.

Another time James got his truck stuck, he had gone out with his friends for one of their birthdays. It was snowing and the wind was blowing. We got a call from James asking us if we could come and pull him out of a snow drift. I asked Jake if he would help, and he looked at me laughing, shaking his head. Josh was also home this time, so he went with us too. We took Jake's Blazer and some chains once again and set out to find James's truck. Snow was already covering the hood; the wind was blowing like crazy, and it was very cold! As Jake and I looked at the guys and the truck, all of us just started laughing. It was funny.

We knew why they were stuck—they were all drunk. I asked Josh if he could drive the truck. He looked at me with what seemed like disagreement in his face and said,

"It's a Ford" and laughed. I looked over at Jake and asked him if he wanted me to drive the Blazer or if he wanted to. He decided he would, and we began to pull the Ford out of the snow. As we got started down the road, Jake ran into some problems. He looked at me and said, "What the heck is Josh doing?" It ended up that Josh had his foot on the brake, keeping Jake from pulling him out. All Jake, Josh, and I could do was stand there and laugh. Like I said before, it always seemed like the boys were always there to help each other out. But this time, they were there not only for James, but for his friends as well.

After an eventful winter, Jake always looked forward to spring because he liked to go fishing. As a family, we went to the other farmer's ponds and lakes, but Jake liked to go to the river with his friend Brian. They would set trout lines and pole fish all night long. After a night full of fishing, he would come home around six thirty or seven in the morning to show his mom and me what he caught. Most of the time, he would bring back some good-sized fish! He would then go out and put them in our pond.

In 1998, Jake's friend John Leroy asked him if he wanted to work at SMH with him. He told Jake that it paid more than he was currently making at the grocery store. Jake went over the pros and cons with him and found there were more positive things about the job than just the pay increase. Jake confronted me about this decision, and we talked about it for a while. I could see that Jake thought it would give him a good chance to do something different. A week later, he took the job with John and seemed to enjoy it. John and Jake took turns driving back and forth to Olathe, where the company was located from then on.

One week in March of 1998, John was late picking up Jake for work. Jake called John's house, and he told him that he had accidentally overslept. He told Jake that he would be there as soon as he could. Jake said not to worry about it and that he would meet John at work. About nine that morning, we received a call from Jake. He told us that while John was pulling out of his driveway, a car hit him on the driver's side and was killed instantly. Jake took John's death very hard. Sara, a good friend of his, joined him at the funeral, which seemed to help a little. She was always there for him if he needed her. John had introduced the two of them; she became his best friend, and they were always together. After several weeks had passed, Jake came to me and told me that he was thinking about joining the army. He said he might join the reserves. It seemed as if the conversation had ended with that, but a few weeks later, he came home and told us that he had joined the army full-time in active duty.

When Jake joined the military, it was not for the money. He went from making around $1,200 to $1,400 a month to making $585 a month with the army. Even though he was going through basic training, he still called home on the weekends. Soon, he was out of basics and was able to come home on some weekends. On some of those weekends, he would take care of his truck and Blazer. He always took the time to wash them by hand, wax them, and clean them out. He was very picky about his trucks.

Jake always liked raising cattle. In the spring of 1997, Jake and I decided to buy some bottle calves; they were all ten to fourteen days old. We knew it was going to take a lot of work to take care of them, and we both had full-time jobs. When we brought the calves home from Wisconsin, Cindy thought we were crazy. Jake and I had kept three of the ten we raised. Jake, Cindy, and I decided to name the three we kept. One was named Bobbit because she had lost part of her tail. Another we named Red because she was a beautiful red color. The third we named Lady because she was pretty, I guess.

One evening, when Jake and I were out taking care of the evening chores of owning calves, we noticed that one was sick. We kept checking on her throughout the night, and she seemed to be doing well; but by morning she was dead. I will never forget the look on Jake's face; it looked lost and empty. He looked as if he had a lot of hurt inside his heart. Jake knew this was a part of life, even though the pain of losing the calf brought tears to his eyes. As time went on, Jake and I would bring more and more calves to the farm. I noticed through time that he would try everything he had to keep each and every one of them healthy and alive. Eventually, Josh started raising calves with us. All three of us had a great time working together even though it was hard work to raise bottle calves.

Jake and I bought our last group of calves around the fourth of July. It was a big mistake because it had gotten too hot, and the calves came down with a disease. The calves came to us on a Friday, and by Sunday, we dug twelve holes. This would be the last group of calves that Jake and I would ever work with together. I just hated that it had to be such a bad experience.

# The Boys and Their Vehicles

When each of the boys were old enough to drive, Cindy and I informed them that they would be responsible for the purchase of a car if they wanted one. We agreed to take them back and forth to work and school until they had enough money to buy one *and* pay for the gas to use it. When each one of our boys saved enough money, we took them out to look at different vehicles around their price range. If they found they didn't have enough money saved for the car they wanted, they saved for a little while longer. We informed our boys that they would be better off starting with an old beater instead of a brand-new car, and they agreed.

One of Jake's first cars was a 1977 Monte Carlo. It was a car that Cindy and I had originally bought for $150. We decided to offer it to Jake, and he gladly accepted it. We lucked out since all three of us were in the market for a car at the time. He continued to save money for a newer car while he worked at the local grocery store. When he had saved enough money for a down payment, he bought a 1986 Trans Am. It took him a year to find that car, but it was exactly what he wanted. It was a beautiful car; it was jet-black with a black interior. The body was perfect; there wasn't a scratch on it!

From the very first day, Jake had problems with that car. Within the first week of owning it, someone had run into it in the grocery store parking lot. A little over a week later, he locked his keys in it. Even before the first payment was made, Jake was rear-ended by a pickup truck while he was taking some friends bowling. This incident totaled the car out completely. Even though he was okay, the paramedics took him to the hospital to check him over. We were worried the whole way up there, but we knew he would be okay. When we arrived, he told us he was "just a little sore." I could feel the relief flow through me. I laughed and said, "Wait until tomorrow! It will be worse than it is right now!"

After the accident, we discussed the need for another vehicle. This time, Jake decided he needed something *bigger* and considered a four-wheel drive. Not long after his accident, he found a full-size 1988 Chevy Blazer. It was nice! It had a two-toned black-over-blue paint job. After he bought it, he put bigger tires on and took it into our back field. He ran it through the mudholes and water, having a blast with his new toy. In the end, it cost over $20 at the car wash to get it clean. All he had to say, *like always*, was "Oh well, I had fun!"

Jake loved all kinds of vehicles. As time went by, he bought newer models. One day when he was home on leave for Christmas, he went to the local Chevy dealer and bought a 2000 Chevy Extreme. It was jet-black and *small*. After asking why he went back to a smaller truck, he explained that the gas was getting too expensive and wanted something with better gas mileage. He never got rid of the Blazer; he left it at our house and drove his 2000 back to Fort Hood, Texas. When Jake was transferred to Fort Riley, he traded in his 2000 Chevy Extreme for a full-size Chevy Z71. He was the happiest he had ever been with this truck!

When I think of Jake's first car, it reminds me of Josh's first car. He had no idea what kind of car he wanted, so I took him to the local junkyard. We walked around the yard for about an hour when a car caught his eye. It was like watching a little kid on Christmas morning opening his presents! He found a 1977 Ford Thunderbird. The motor in it was no good, and it needed a new transmission. Even with all the work that it had to have done, he still wanted it. Along with the car, we also found a motor and transmission. He was able to buy all three for $150! We loaded everything on our trailer and took it back to the house so Josh could start working on it. Naturally, Jake and James took an interest in fixing it as well. With all three of them working on it, they had it running and on the road in about a week.

Josh drove it for about six months and sold it for $1250. He then took the money he had made and bought a 1977 Chevy pickup truck. This truck ended up causing a lot of problems. One day when Josh was visiting his girlfriend, the truck came out of gear and rolled down the hill it was parked on and crashed through the front of his girlfriend's house! Josh was lucky no one was hurt! As we stood back and assessed the damage, we all had a good laugh. I have always told my boys that things can be put together and replaced, but a life cannot.

# Family and Friends

As my family has gone down the roads of life, I have seen two types of roads. Some people are lucky enough to get the smooth road; they seem to glide along. The other road seems to be rough with a lot of bumps and dips. My family has seen both roads, more of the rough road it seems, but they never complain. I think it's because of our love for God and our faith in Him that makes the road appear to be smoother. Our family knows that the time we have on this earth is only for a short time, and it should be happy. Even though life seems simple, it's true.

It was 1997 when my mom and dad decided to build a retirement home. They would visit about three to four times a week to work on plans for the house. It took almost a year before the plans were complete and up to par with exactly what they wanted. We finally started working on their house in June of 1998. All of us worked very hard to get to that point, and we were finally *there* putting it together. James and Josh worked with me, and my brothers Rob and Karl also worked with us every day. My dad helped out when he could. Joe and Jake helped every day after they had finished working at their regular jobs. We worked almost every weekend, but no one seemed to mind because we were all working together. After the house was finished, my parents were ecstatic. This was the first home they had ever built. As a family, we were all happy to be involved in this part of my mom and dad's life *and* to have done it together as a family.

As I am writing this, winter has come again. As I sit on the couch and look out the sliding glass door, I see that winter has put ice on the ground and trees and everything it could touch. I know the branches are strong without ice on them, but the extra weight makes them seem so fragile. The tree branches remind me of family. If they are bumped or strained, the branches will break. This is similar to when there is a great deal of stress on a family. If they are hit with more stress, they could break. Yet as the ice melts and spring begins, new growth will appear. In a family, this is like coming through hard times and moving forward. Nature is similar to human life. The only difference is that nature moves faster.

# Family Times

When the boys were growing up, we took several trips to Minnesota where part of Cindy's family lived. One year, her sister invited us to go tubing down the Apple River. Let me clarify what her idea of tubing was. We took a big inner tube, which is a large donut-shaped float, and we sat in the hole in the middle with our legs and top halves hanging over the sides. We floated down the river, letting the currents take us slowly downstream. The ride took about three hours and was really relaxing and fun. As we got to the end of the river, we saw an area of rapids. You had a choice to either get out before the rapids or go through them. Jake and his brothers decided to brave the rapids, but Cindy and I chose to get out. Right after that ride, they ended up taking another ride to the local hospital in an ambulance. Luckily for them, they ended up only suffering some minor cuts and bruises!

Some of the fun our family has experienced together was at the casino. The first time Cindy and I ever went to a casino was when Joe and Jake gave us a $120 gift certificate to a local casino as a Christmas gift. After Jake joined the army, our visits became few and far between. However, when Jake made his way back into town, Cindy, Joe, Jake, and I would go have some fun at the casino. Cindy always got jealous of Joe and Jake because they always seemed to win something! They just had a lucky side to them. Jake and I would have a few drinks, and we would talk about women or other things going on in our lives. These talks always ended up in laughter. Laughter and teasing each other is what our family is all about. Yet we all know that there are times to be serious and take care of business.

Justin, our youngest boy, was born with spina bifida. Cindy and I knew he would have a lot of medical needs and that he would need the support of his brothers. Jake and the other boys ended up spending a lot of time in the hospital as Justin was growing up, but they always had smiles on their faces and were always there to support him. One summer, Justin had more problems than usual and had three close calls with death. Jake was always the one that would worry the most about Justin. He was always there to lend support to his mom and his brother.

Even now that Jake is not here with us, the family continues to support each other in good and bad times. Our family remains united. Throughout the seasons and holidays, Jake is still here in spirit. The holidays are not easy with him gone. If I were able to hear him, I believe he would say, "Remember the simple things in life, and someday, we will be together again." He would remind the family not to forget about the love they have for each other. Jake has left us some beautiful memories. Every time I visit Jake's grave, the memories he has given me come flooding back. He may be gone, but he will never be forgotten by his family or the other lives he touched.

# We Will Always Remember

Jake and I liked to spend time together. Whenever we had a chance, we would sit out by the pond. One day, we watched a group of doves flying in. At this moment, I felt the need to tell Jake that I had been tired lately. I asked him to look around and tell me what he saw, if he could tell me if he thought it was peaceful. I reminded him that we are all here on earth for a short time and that he should enjoy life to its fullest. Everything we have here is material; everything but our love for each other. That is the most important thing we could ever possess. He just looked at me and smiled. We sat there for a little while longer watching the doves and then headed back to the house.

I will forever remember that as one of the special times I spent as just the two of us.

As I look at the people in the United States today, I notice how attached everyone is to the material things. They are forgetting the simple things in life such as the love and care we have for one another. This is something that doesn't cost a thing but can be the most priceless thing you will ever have. I will always remember each and every one of all my sons' first smiles and laughs. I remember the first time they rolled over, their first steps, and when they first started talking. I remember as the boys grew up, they would fight and laugh with each other. We never got onto them too much about fighting because we both knew that the boys would need these skills to make it in the real world. As we get older, things get more complex. We need to remember back when we were young and the love we felt for each other; never let that die! My love and care for my family goes very deep into my soul, and I would do whatever it takes to protect my family, even if it meant putting my life on the line.

Around the holidays, my birthday, and Father's Day, the boys had always asked me what I wanted. I would always give them the same answer: "I don't want anything. I just want all of you here with me." At Christmas, James and Jake would help me put the Christmas lights on the house. Joe, Josh, and Justin always thought it needed more, so Jake would wrap all the poles around our front porch with lights.

Ever since Jake died, I haven't been able to find it in myself to put all the lights up. It's not the same without Jake here. This year, Cindy tried to cheer me up. She told me that the grandchildren were still around and would enjoy the lights. I decided that *maybe* next year would be better. The worst part about this Christmas was that the whole family was not together. It seemed as if the family was starting to drift apart. I sometimes wonder if we will ever be as close as we were when Jake was alive.

Jake was always a very social person. Whenever he was on the job site with his grandfather and me, he met all kinds of different people. He learned a great deal from those relationships. He had so much fun meeting new people that work became more fun and interesting. Jake told me several times that when he got out of the army, he would like to work with me. I told him every time that I would be honored to have him as a partner.

When Jake was around, he would always be busy; he could never just sit and do nothing. Jake and Josh went hunting for deer one weekend when he was in town. They would wear their orange vests or sweatshirts. They came back to the house after being out for a long time and walked in rubbing their hands together. They stood there just looking at me. With a smile, I asked Jake if he thought it was that cold outside. With a big grin, he said, " Heck yeah!" It wasn't like them to be back from hunting so early, so I inquired as to why. Jake informed me, "Because there are crazy people out there! While we were in the field waiting for the deer to get close to us, some guy came running through, shooting from behind us!" Needless to say, he didn't get his deer that day.

In the winter of 2003, Jake, James, Josh, and I went out to cut wood. It was actually more fun than work because while we worked, we talked and caught up with each other. We would get two truckloads of wood cut and brought back to the house to split without even realizing we had put in a full day of work!

I remember how much Jake loved to work on things with his brothers. James and Josh had a load of things to take to the dump one day, so the three of them made the trip together. While they were there, they found two battery-operated four-wheelers. They brought them back to the house and tried to put the two together to make one. When Jake came home for the weekend, he helped his brothers with pulling the pieces apart and then putting them back together. By the time they were finished, they had a running battery-operated four-wheeler! They painted it up, and when it was finished, they decided to give it to James's son, Jess.

Not long after Jake returned from his second tour of duty in Kuwait, he was called for training again. His platoon was going to the Mojave Desert for desert training. When he told his mother and me about this, he was not happy about it. He couldn't understand why they needed to go to the desert for training since they just got back from six months in the desert. He was getting burned out, and he needed a break from it. He wasn't alone; the majority of his platoon felt the same way. When he was there, he was able to come into the main base and call us. He just so happened to call on the day that the space shuttle *Columbia* had exploded. That day reminded me of when we took him and his brother's to see the *Columbia* space shuttle; it came through the Kansas City Airport. All the boys stood there looking at the shuttle in awe. I wonder if Jake remembered that.

It is sometimes interesting how music is such a big part of our lives. Jake listened to all kinds of music. We would listen to Steve Earl and other country oldies. Jake related to some songs, like Allan Jackson's "Little Bitty." There were several songs that meant a lot to Jake, his mom, and I. One song was "Darlin' Be Home Soon" by the Lovin' Spoonful.

# Going into the Army

In the fall of 1998, Jake got very excited; it was getting close for him to go to boot camp. Cindy and I decided to give him a going-away party. We figured bringing in some barbeque, beer, and friends would give him support. We both knew it was going to be a rough time for him, and we knew he needed all the love and support he could get from his family and friends. He could have made it through just fine without the extra support, but it probably made things easier.

The day Jake had signed his papers to join the army, he came home and told me that he weighed in at 109 pounds. He needed to weigh at least 110 pounds. It was amusing to see him eat. In less than a week, he had that extra pound on board. That goes to show how determined and serious he was about joining the army. He wasn't going to let anything get in his way. As I looked at Jake before his going-away party, I could see the effects of a good mother. I could tell we had done a good job raising him. He had turned into a nice young man that his mother and I could not be more proud of!

While Jake was in boot camp, he called us whenever he could. Sometimes he sounded upset, but after a few months, I finally understood why. For his age, he was under a great deal of mental and physical stress. When we went to see him graduate from boot camp, we noticed a lot of young men walking around on crutches. We had to know why. Jake wouldn't say anything, but we finally got a glimpse of just how much physical strain these young men and women had to endure.

The night after Jake's graduation, he was given permission to ride back from Kentucky to Kansas with his family. He was home for a short time. He had to leave for Fort Hood, Texas, where he would be stationed for the next eighteen months.

While he was in Texas, he would call whenever he got time. When he was able to get leave, he would come home and spend time with the family. When he called, he would always ask how everyone was doing and about the farm and cattle. One time, I remember telling him I had just had a cow butchered. He replied, "Great! I'll be coming home this weekend, and maybe we can have some steaks!" I just laughed; that sounded great!

Later that year, in 1999, Jake came into town for the Fourth of July weekend. He showed up just as I was digging the footings for the new room addition. As Jake got out of his truck, he asked me what I was doing. I sat on the backhoe and looked at him with a smile. I said, "Your mom wanted a room addition, so she's getting one." Later that year, Jake took his first tour of duty in Kuwait. While there, he called and wrote letters; there wasn't Skype back then. He told us over and over how hot it was and how the air-conditioned tents were ninety to ninety-five degrees. He also told us how the flies were bad, along with the fleas and other desert critters. He usually ended all the calls and letters with how he couldn't wait to come home.

While Jake was deployed, Cindy would tie a big yellow ribbon around our oak tree. Then when he came home, she would hand him a pair of scissors and stand next to him as he cut the ribbon. They would share a big hug after he took it down.

Later that year, after Jake returned to the States and settled in at Fort Hood, Cindy, Joe, Justin, and I went to see him. He was so happy to see his family; he spent the whole day showing us around the base. After showing us around, he mentioned going to Corpus Christi. He wanted to walk on the beach. It didn't take much to persuade us, so we all loaded up and headed to the beach. As Joe and Jake walked down the beach barefoot, I could see how much they meant to each other as brothers and as friends. We were only there for a couple of days, but those are some of the memories I remember fondly. This was the only time we got to see him at Fort Hood.

Time passed by, and eventually Jake decided he wanted to be closer to the family, especially his two beloved nieces, Shelby and Kaitlyn. He chose to transfer to Fort Riley, Kansas, which allowed him to come home more frequently. He wanted to be around his family no matter what was going on. If I was away on a job, he would stop by and help out to get the job done. He was the type of person that never took a vacation. He may have taken a couple days off to go fishing, but he never took what most would consider a vacation. When Jake and I spent some time alone, we talked about his brothers and how they were all doing. He would always ask me how his mom and I were doing; he was always concerned and interested in what was happening in our lives.

Not long after Jake had transferred to Fort Riley, he found out that he would be going back to Kuwait for Operation Desert Spring 02–02. He would be gone again for about six months. Again, we went through the process of waiting for letters and phone calls. We sent him care packages every two weeks; he loved them because they contained all of his necessities, such as fresh cigarettes, Kool-Aid (to add flavor to his water), and smoked oysters. The oysters were not really for him; he told us that the other guys liked them.

When he came home from Kuwait the second time, he immediately called us to come pick him up. If he could get block leave, he could stay home for about a week. When we arrived at Fort Riley, he was excited to see us. He was always geared up and ready to go home, and we were excited to see him as well!

This time when Jake came home, it was on the weekend that Josh came over to the house to shoot skeet. This is when you put clay pigeons or saucers in a machine and sling them into the air as you shoot them. Josh set up a target, and we used his 30/30 gun for target practice. The boys all laughed as they missed the target and broke the barbed wire fence. They may have laughed for a while, but eventually, they would be helping me fix it!

# Josh, Chrissy, and Jake's Nieces

n 1998, Josh and Chrissy decided to get married. They chose the front porch of our house to say their vows. They worked so hard to get everything together. All the bridesmaids were chosen, and Josh made James his best man. All the boys were there for the wedding except James; no one knew where he was. Jake pulled me and jokingly whispered, "I think James took the wedding more seriously than Josh!" It's funny now, but at the time, it seemed like James had let Josh down on one of the biggest days of his life. As I watched Josh and Chrissy exchange vows, it reminded me of when Cindy and I got married. I wished then, and still hope today, that they will have a happy marriage like Cindy and I have had.

It wasn't long after they were married that grandchildren came. The firstborn was a beautiful little girl, Shelby. Cindy was so excited that she was the first girl to join the family. A few years later, another baby girl joined our family: Kaitlyn. We call her KK. Jake loved those little girls more than anything I had ever seen him love. He tried to spend as much time with them as he possibly could. On President's Day weekend in 2003, Jake was on leave for the whole weekend. We were all sitting around the house having a good time when the phone rang. The military was on the other end. They ordered Jake to return to Fort Riley as soon as he could. They were told to get all their things loaded on the trains and head out. After the call, Jake told me he wasn't going anywhere until he saw his nieces. I took him to Josh and Chrissy's house so he could say good-bye. As Jake was holding KK tight, tears came down his face. I started toward him to let him know that we should be leaving soon, but he just held up his hand and told me that he wanted a little more time.

When we left, he told me that when he gets out of the military, he wanted to buy some land and build a house. He wanted to start his own family. Jake had a greater love for his family than most people realize. It hurts to think that Jake was never able to fulfill his dreams of having a family.

# Saying Good-Bye

t was a call that parents of a soldier never want to receive. Jake called us on March 1, 2003, and informed us he was going to be deploying to Iraq. We were concerned because we knew Jake was going to be in harm's way. We called Jake's grandparents, Robert and Nancy, and asked if they wanted to go to Fort Riley to say good-bye. The same call was also made to Josh and his family. I emphasized the importance of them going with us because I knew deep down that this might be the last time we would see Jake.

On the way there, we picked up his grandparents. Jake's sister in-law, Chrissy, and his niece, Kaitlyn, followed behind. We arrived at around one in the afternoon and met up with Jake to spend time as a family. After a while, Jake showed us around the base; he wanted us to see what he did and where he worked. We all crammed into Chrissy's minivan and took a drive. Then we went to Walmart and Radio Shack so Jake could pick up some last-minute things he needed to take with him to Iraq.

That night, all of us had dinner at the Cracker Barrel. Everyone was eating and enjoying themselves, but I noticed Jake didn't seem to eat much. He ordered a blackberry cobbler with vanilla ice cream and a glass of Coke; he normally eats more than that. It was obvious that his nerves were tense about going overseas, about going to war. As we walked out to the parking lot to say our last good-byes, everyone was laughing and joking around, trying to make the moment less tense. At about that time, James and his son, Jess, along with Joe, Jake's twin, pulled into the parking lot. They decided to visit Jake for the evening.

Jake said good-bye to his grandma, grandpa, Chrissy, Kaitlyn, and his mom. As I walked Jake to his truck, we talked about his departure. I will never forget the details of that night for as long as I live. The sky was lit up with the brightest stars, and the air was brisk with not a cloud in sight. I embraced Jake in one last hug, and told him, "I love you. If you use common sense and the training that you learned, you will come home safe." Although all the training in the world would not have saved him the day he died. I just stood there looking at him, and his eyes were red from the tears rolling down his pale cheeks. This was the first sign of the fear he was so desperately trying to hide. I began to cry with him. As I wiped the tears from my cheeks,

I assured him that I loved him and pleaded with him to be safe. Yet I still could not help but think of the inevitable. I knew that if what Jake, as well as I, dreamt about the past few months came true, my son would not be coming home to me. Instead, he would be going to live with God.

With all the good-byes said and tears shed, we headed back home. James, Jess, and Joe stayed to visit for a while longer. Jake took them on base to his barracks where they dressed Jess, then two years old, in Jake's army fatigues and took pictures. They had a great time with Jake that night.

As the war in Iraq was about to begin, Cindy and I watched the news every day, wanting to know what was happening. On March 19, 2003, the war in Iraq began. We could not find out where Jake was or what part of the war he was involved in. Before he left, he told me that he thought he would be guarding the prisoners of war (POWs) or that he would be cleaning up after the first front went through the area. Several days had passed since Jake had left. Time seemed like it was going in slow motion. Then finally, on March 28, we received a phone call from him. We were beyond happy to hear his voice! We didn't even care that it was three thirty in the morning. He told us he was in Iraq, but he couldn't say where. As his mom was talking to him, she asked him if he needed toilet paper. He laughed and replied, "How did you know?" She laughed and said she had heard it through the grapevine. They were both in great spirits laughing and joking. After they were done talking, I got on the phone. As we talked, I could hear a quiver in his voice. I said, "I love you, Jake. Come home soon." As I hung up the phone that night, I had no idea that it would be the last time I would ever hear his voice again. It would be the last time I would hear him laugh.

We found out later that the last phone call we received was from a satellite phone. Jake used it when he was close to an air base his platoon had taken over. Cindy and I will never forget how *thankful* we were that we got to hear from our son that *one last time*.

When you grow older, you expect the fact that you will lose your parents. I know it's not easy; however, you never expect to lose a child. Parents are not supposed to outlive their children. As we were sitting together, Cindy told me that she felt like it is harder to lose your child than a parent. Jake is a part of *us* that can't ever be replaced. As the days go by, Cindy and I still feel the hurt and pain from the loss of our son, but we will never forget him. We will continue to stay strong because of our love for God and his son Jesus Christ.

I know all our boys will look back, as they have since Jake has passed, and remember all the good and bad times this family has gone through and never forget their love for each other.

Dear mom and Dad
How is everything? I am fine
still just seating hear doing the
same thing as last time. That Radio
that we built has come in to be
really handy we have Leasoned to
it every day. we got the New
Address it is

  SGT Butler Jacob
  HHC 1-41 IN
  18th MP BDE
  APO AE 09302-1300

Con you tell everyone for me, we still
don't know our mission over hear. Some
say that we will go up and secure a
airlase up North Others say we
will be following the main force.
and getting everyone that they missed.
No one really know what we are doing.
there is alot of people hear more than
I have ever saw Before in one place with
gun's and ammo. Well I better go got
some thing's to do. Love you
                          Love.
                          Jake

3-18-03

Jake.

Miss ya so much. Love ya so much. Please hurry home your fathers Hair is driving me crazy.

I know this is what you trained for. I know this is what you want to do. Please know that we support you 100% and we lose sleep worrying about your safety. We pray for you to come back safe + sound to us. I'm sorry I just love you so much and don't want anything to happen to you.

We got your letter today it was postmarked the 9th and today is the 18th. Not Bad for the Post office. Dad's Busy working on the kitchen James is filling the dumpster Justin is sitting in his truck so not much going on around here. Grampa + Gramma stopped by and I gave them your address. He wanted me to send you these pictures
                            Love,
                               Mom

Dear mom and Dad

How is everyone? I am fine, Hope
you got my last letter. They said
we could have packages but they are
not priority. My Stereo burned up the
other day. can you send me another
one. The stereo for my box anyways.
and they have hardly any cigaretes over
hear So can you send one carton every
package or as much as you can.
And can you send some of those
Small padded envelops. The rumma is
now that we may be back home
about mid June or early July. But plan
on Dec some time. They still don't
Know when we are going to do this.
There is so many dates up in the air.
We got our mission so far it ain't
that bad at least to the point were we
won't be in that much contact. Well
better go. Love you.

Love Jake

Dear Mom and Dad

How is everything and everyone? I am fine. We are now just seating hear waiting. Mom I wanted to thank you a lot for taking care of my bills. If you could save me as much money as you can. I also wrote a check the other day for $40.00. They have a PX hear but they are always out of shit. and the line is hours long. They have phones hear to but the line is usely 3 to 4 hours long and we usely don't have that much time to seat and wait so sorry if I don't call that much. They still don't know what the fuck is going on around hear. you guys know more with CNN than we will know. There is so many reports over hear. Did you guys get the house done or where you can live in it at least? Today the 16 mar we have to go me with the special forces on some of the mission's we will do. Well I have got to go so we can do this shit. Love you

Love Jake

Dear mom and Dad

How is everyone and everything? I am fine.
Sorry I have wrote as much as I should but
we have been real busy. Happy Birthday Mom
Sorry I was not there. Can you tell everyone
the reason why I have not wrote that
much. We moved North from Talel Q to
Asamawha or something like that we have
been hear for about 3 days. We had to
escort some people up North yesterday
the 31st of march and we got in to the
Shit up there It was really bad but we
all walked out ok. I have never seen so
many Dead people in one area in my life.
well I really don't want to talk about that
any more we still have not got any
mail they said we have mail but It
is all in Kuwait Still Just Sestting
there It is really pissing us all off
they said something about we may leave
in may sometime but don't count on
it. we are all hoping and praying we
do. It was really nice to call you
the other day I wish I could do that
more. The other day we had a car bombing
that killed 5 US. Soldiers that really pissed
us all off. on the 30th SGT Heller which is

63

One of our Scout and a really good
friend got life lited out becous they
were driving and hit some thick dust
well some one else was comeing the
other way and they did not see each
other well they hit head on and
toteled out his truck. He is going
to be fine just some stiches thats all
but other then that no one in the Scout
Pltoon has been hurt. He was life lite
down to taleto where they have the
MASH which is the field hospdel
He was telling me what he saw and I
don't want to repeated I was so bad. Tell
everyone I am o fine and I love them
give my huges and kisses to the girls and
Jess. I guess they are going to
attach Bygdaball sometime in the next couple
of days. It is going like we will not
be there for that because we are still
300 km South of there which is fine
with me. I just want this shit to
get over with. well got to go love
you, miss you.
                          Love Jake

Dear mom and Dad
  How are you? I am fine. Today
is 20 march 03 our time is 1:30 in
the after noon your time it will be
4:30 in the morning. Iraq just fired
2 scuds at us and 2 at Kuwait City
It Look Like the war is going to
start. I am sorry that I did not
call or write that much. They said that
we will not get mail or be able
to mail mail out for 7 days but
I will write in this letter every day.
well today is Day 2 of the war
and we already earned our combat
patch. write now we are Just
setting waiting on permission to
move farther north. The marines are
moving really quick with little to
No resistance. The Chopper that went
down Iguess they figured out that
it wasnt do to enemy. In the middle
of the night Iraq fired more scuds at
us but not close to us. I Just want
to get this shit over with and go
home. The Flys are really bad here
and they drive me nuts. Well its day
3 and we have be up sense we crossd

The Burm. we really have not seen much just 3 tanks that is it we are almost up to the air field I guess that is wear 3rd ID has hit the most resecestance we are sopost to take over the air field for them, They said that we do that tomorrow. You know I never thought that I would Say that I helped make history. And I don't know why anyone would want to live in this god forsaken place of a country we have drove for 2 strate days and have not seen a town or Nothing. Well Its day 4 and we are getting ready to go to Taleto Air Field I guess that is where the shit is but we will find out in a few hours. Well Its day 5 and we finaly made it to the Airfield and took it over. we are sopost to keep pushing but No one knows how far and when It will probably be today Sometime. as I was writing this 2 medivac choppers came in and they droped off 1 Enemy Dead and 1 Enemy that Burned really Bad but Still alive and the other chopper had 5 friendly wounded all were sopost to Live. well its Day 6

Yesterday we destoryd 2 artillery peaces
and abunch of rounds. Today we are
sopost to destroy 2 more and abunch of
rounds. They said that there is 1 enemy
Company of infantry on its way to
the air field but No sign of them
yet. Well got to go So I can send
this Letter off. I love you

Love Jake

P.S. Don't worry about me.
I will be Fine

# Dreams

am not sure if everyone has dreams like I have had throughout the years or if it is just something that only I experience. About two years before Jake was killed, I started to have a reoccurring dream; it continued for months. In this dream, I would see different people's faces, people I had never seen in my life. It wasn't just one or two people that I saw; it was thousands of people's faces. They would range from people that looked like they were from this time to people that were dressed as if they were from the 1800s. All the people I saw in my dreams were adults, men and women of various ages with different hairstyles. They seemed to be from all different backgrounds; some seemed to have a great deal of money by the way they were dressed. Some seemed like they had nothing but their family. There were women that had all kinds of jewelry, all of which were fancy and beautiful. Some women were wearing only dirty rags for clothes. The men looked exactly the same way as the women did. I didn't know what to think of this dream, nor do I know what to think about it now.

About six months before Jake was killed, the dream changed. The faces I saw in my dream were faces of people I had known, friends and family that had died throughout my life. I didn't know what this dream meant. I still don't know. I wouldn't say anything about the dreams to Cindy or the kids. I was worried they might think I was crazy. Three months before Jake was killed, I had yet another dream. I was looking at six different people; they didn't have faces this time. As the dream went on, I noticed they were carrying a casket. I had this dream several times, and the six people never had faces until the day of Jake's funeral. It was then that I realized the dream was about the six people we would have to pick to be pallbearers.

I didn't know for some time, but Jake was having similar dreams. Both of us had a tough time telling the family about them. They did not understand that these were not like regular dreams; they were much different.

In Jake's dream, his best friend who was killed in the car accident in 1998, John, came to him and told him it was time for him to come live with him and God. Jake refused to talk about his dream for a long time. I could understand because I was dealing with the same thing. We were both being faced by a world that believed dreams were just made up; to believe something like that was crazy. I think the reason why most people believe this way is because they have not had dreams such as ours.

It was not only the dreams; I noticed other signs as well. I truly believe that if people would slow down and pay attention, they would see signs such as I did. Back when Jake and I brought the first group of calves to the farm, Jake became attached to Bobbit and Red. About a month before Jake was to leave for Iraq, we found out that Bobbit was pregnant and was going to have twins. I told this to Cindy, but she thought I was full of it. Jake would just laugh because he knew it was true. About a week before Jake left, Bobbit had her calves. I was away at work when Cindy called me to come home. When I pulled into the driveway, Cindy was already in the field with Bobbit. The first calf born died right away, but the second calf lived. Most people would not take notice of this, but after Jake's death, I look back on that day and see it as a sign. Jake was a twin, and just five weeks after Bobbit gave birth, he lost his life. Only one twin was left.

Sometimes I think about the dream Jake had of John before he went to Iraq. I know it must have been hard to keep all of the feelings he had from his dream deep inside. I knew he was afraid that if he told me or anyone else, we would tell him to forget about it. But that's not what he needed to hear.

I remember the first dream I had when I was sixteen. In it, I saw everything that happened on the day my brother, three friends, and I were coming back from a fishing trip. As we headed back from Desoto, Kansas, on K-10 highway, we noticed there was slow traffic due to construction on the highway. My brother, who was driving, was trying to beat the traffic and get in front of all the slowdowns. He decided to take an exit ramp and take the entrance ramp back onto the highway before the other cars reached it. A car that was heading north on the road we were crossing hit us at a high speed. When the car struck, I happened to look out the window and saw the woman's head come through the windshield. As I turned and looked out the front window, I could see a semitruck heading toward us. It was loaded with highway construction signs and equipment and likely very heavy. Everything seemed to be moving in slow motion as we went under the trailer. I heard the windshield break, and at that moment, it seemed like everything sped up. The motor of our car was stuck as if someone was pushing on the gas pedal, so my brother shut the car off. This sound let me know he was still alive. I opened the car door on the passenger side to climb out. When I was able to free myself, I realized I had blood all over me. That was when a horrible pain shot up from my hand; somehow, I had cut one of my fingers off.

I had seen all of this happen in my dream, but no one had believed my warnings when I told them about it. I would like to say my dreams are premonitions. Since Jake had his dream, I feared it would have the same outcome mine always had: actual truth. I always hoped that none of our boys would have dreams like me. Hopefully Jake will be the only one to have them. He was a little older than I was when I had my first dream; I can remember thinking about how much of a burden knowing things seemed to be. Now that I continue to have them, I have learned to deal with them by just taking life one day at a time.

Since Jake's death, the dreams seemed to fade, but they started to happen again. One dream was of a man who was in his middle to late thirties. In my dream, we would always stand looking at each other with no emotions. His hair was shoulder length, wavy, and dark brown, and he had a full beard and mustache. His eyes were big and brown; they felt very cold. Even though I could see the man and all the details of him, we never exchanged words in any of the dreams. To this day, I have not been able to figure out who this man is or what the dream is trying to tell me.

I still had one dream that was concerning to me, but didn't talk about it to anyone until Lieutenant Colonel Chaplain Thomas discussed it with me. One evening, Captain Roach contacted me and told me he was concerned about my plans as well as the dreams. I didn't say much to him, but he was serious enough that he contacted Lt. Col. Chaplain Thomas because the next thing I know, Captain Roach was asking me if the chaplain can come to visit with me.

Later that day, they came to the house. After visiting, the chaplain asked me if I was doing okay. I was, but I mentioned that I would like to talk to her about my dreams in private. We walked outside, and I started to tell her. She was able to keep the tension lowered by occasionally talking about the farm and the cattle. We finally stopped walking and sat down on a little hill under the tree in our backyard. She was concerned about the dreams, but I told her that they didn't really bother me. I just wished I could understand them better. We talked a little while longer, and then she asked me if we could say a prayer. I was more than willing to oblige and felt better afterward.

Two days after the chaplain and Captain Roach came over, I had another dream. In this dream, I was looking at a wall that was covered in green foliage. In the middle of the wall, there was a gold cross that was so bright; it seemed to give off light. Below the cross was a casket. It seemed to be made of wood, and it was closed. As I looked to the left of the casket, there were three men all dressed in white robes looking at me. All three men had wavy hair and brown beards. The man in the middle was a little taller than the others. He looked at me through his big eyes, and all of the sudden, I felt a warm, peaceful feeling spread throughout my body. He then stretched his arms out toward me with his palms up, like he was inviting me to go with him.

Since these dreams and the visit I had with the chaplain, I have had several more of the same nature. I can't tell if

God is trying to help me understand something or if he is trying to tell me something else. In a recent dream, I was standing on my back deck, looking toward the sky. There is a large area in the sky with clouds rolling toward me. The bottoms of the clouds are black; above those are clouds that were the brightest color of red I have ever seen. It was not the sun making this magnificent color because the sun was above all the clouds. The only thing I know from this dream is that the year was 2007. At first, I had trouble understanding why I was only getting the year. But then I started thinking about what the chaplain had said in our prayer together. She had asked God to help me understand the dreams and to bless the cattle. The other thing I saw in this dream is in that year 2007, Cindy and I had fifty-one heads of cattle die. The odd thing was I would be fifty-one in 2007.

With all the dreams I've had, I have had several about Jake. In one, Jake and I were hugging. As I looked over Jake's shoulder, there was a little boy. I noticed the little boy had blond hair, and he had tears rolling down his cheeks; he had a scratch on one of his cheeks. While looking at the little boy, I could feel the pain he was feeling. After that dream, I found a picture of Jake when he was five years old, and he looked just like the little boy in my dream.

# April Fool's Day

It was April 1, 2003. Everything was the same around our house. James, Cindy, and I were watching the news, keeping an eye on what was going on in Iraq. The 10:30 p.m. news broadcast just finished for the evening, and Cindy and James were headed to bed. I was not sleeping well, so I decided to stay up and watch television for a little while longer. At 10:40 p.m., I heard a car pull in the driveway and heard two car doors shut. I listened to the footsteps coming up the stairs of the deck and knew, right then, it was not going to be good news. I looked toward the sliding glass door and saw two officers from the army standing on the front porch. My stomach suddenly felt empty. As I got up from the couch and slowly walked to the door, I noticed it seemed like my feet were stuck in mud, and I was struggling to get to the door. As I opened the door and looked into their faces, I asked, "Is he hurt bad, or is he dead?" The chaplain hung her head down, and I knew. I stepped back and let them in.

As I walked toward the bedroom to get Cindy, I thought to myself about the promise I made to Jake and how I was going to keep that promise. I promised to go to Iraq if something happened to him. I had to keep it; this was my last promise to my son. I walked into the bedroom and toward the light switch and turned it on. I looked at Cindy lying there asleep so peacefully. I sat on the edge of the bed and laid my hand on her arm and spoke softly, "Cindy…Cindy." She opened her eyes and looked at me. My heart filled with sorrow as I told my wife that her son had been killed in Iraq. She raised her voice and said, "It's not supposed to be this way!" And she started crying. I knew at that moment that I was going to have to stand strong to help my family stay together.

I asked her to come with me to the next room to talk to the chaplain. Cindy looked at me with desperation in her eyes and said, "It's not funny if this is an April Fool's joke." With a heavy heart, I looked her in the eyes and told her it wasn't a joke. As I walked back into the living room where the inevitable waited, I called up the stairs to James and told him he should come down.

That night, as the military officers were talking to us about Jake, they could only say that he was killed with a rocket-propelled grenade (RPG). The chaplain and the other officer left after a couple of hours and said that more military personnel would be out the next day. Cindy, James, and I were discussing what to do next when Cindy realized she had run out of her medication. I knew she was a nervous wreck, so I called Donna, our local pharmacist, at home. I told her what was going on, and she asked me to meet her at the pharmacy so she could get Cindy the medicine she needed. It makes a person feel good when you know that there are good-hearted people around like Donna.

As we headed to the pharmacy, I thought about how we needed to get to the rest of the family; we needed to get together so we could be there for each other and stand strong together. I knew in my heart this is what Jake would have wanted us to do. I did not want any of the family to hear about Jake on the local news; they needed to hear it from us.

Cindy, James, and I drove into town where Joe lived. It was one thirty in the morning as we gathered outside Joe's apartment door. As I knocked on the door, I couldn't believe Jake was really gone. I could see the hurt and pain in Cindy's and James's faces as we stood outside, waiting patiently. With another knock on the door, Joe's roommate, Ed, greeted us. I asked if Joe was there, and he let us in. We walked back to Joe's bedroom and turned on the light. As Cindy and I told Joe, I could feel his pain and anguish as he started to cry. After we sat and talked for a while, I told them that we needed to get to the other family members.

We were running out of time, and it was getting close to morning; it would be all over the news.

We then headed back south where Josh and Chrissy's family lived. After knocking on their door several times and calling their phone, Josh came down to answer the door. We told the news to Josh, then he went up to get Chrissy, and we told them together. We left Shelby and Kaitlyn asleep; they would find out the terrible news in the morning.

We did not know where Justin, Jake's youngest brother, was, so we drove to my mom and dad's house to tell them their grandson had been killed. They took the news as well as any grandparents receiving the news of the death of their grandchild would. Walking out of their house, I listened to the birds singing and knew that it was getting close to sunrise. We went from Baldwin back to Wellsville because one of the boys thought they knew where Justin might be; I guess they knew their brother better than I did. We found him and told him the news around five thirty in the morning. Now the whole family knew, and we all would be able to be together for the day. I was glad we were able to tell the family ourselves. It was important to me that they not hear about Jake's death for the first time on television.

Dear mom and Dad
    If you are reading this that means
that I did not make it. I Just wanted
to say that I love you very much and don't
for get me because we will meet again
I will tell everyone in heaven Hellow and
you Love to them. I am Sorry that I
put you through so much greate and gsaney
Sorry I can't spell. I need you to do
Something for me Dad I want you to
take some of my Life Insurance money
and raise those Calf Like you want to
and mom take Some of the money and
Buy you a brane New Car or truck what
every you want and Both of you take
about 30 thousand and open a savings
acount for HH, Shelby, and Jesse So
when they get older they have money for
collage, and last but not Least finish
the house and pay it off and retire, off and
give grandma and grandpa some money to.
and Jamie, Justin, Joe, Josh, Chrissy, Jess, Shelby,
HH I love you don't forget me,
        we will all meet again Some day
            Love you
                Love Jake

# The Unknown

After Jake was killed, all his mother and I wanted to know was *how* he died. All the military was able to tell us was that he was killed by a rocket-propelled grenade (RPG). Even though we found out later that they knew, after the third day, how he was *really* killed. Many terrible things went through our minds. Was our son coming back to us in one piece? Was he hit directly by the RPG? Would there be anything left of him? We found out he was killed by a gunshot wound to the head when his body arrived at the Wellsville Funeral Home. I had told Cindy previously that I wanted to see Jake one last time. I had to see him. I told her that she did not have to be there when the funeral director opened the casket. Cindy looked at me with sadness in her eyes and said, "I want to see him one last time. I want to touch him and hold his hand." When we opened the casket, I looked at Cindy. She was looking at him with tears streaming down her cheeks. She reached down and took her son's hand in hers for the last time.

Before Jake's body came back to the United States, the military told us that none of his body would be available for viewing. After that, they said that only *part* of his body would be viewable. We didn't know what to expect; we were confused and lost. When Jake's platoon came back from Iraq, some of the soldiers told us he was shot twice.

From all the information we were getting from different sources, we didn't know what to believe. Cindy and I had a lot bigger things to take care of, such as where we would have Jake's funeral services and where he would be buried. We asked the superintendent of the local high school if we could have the services there because that was where Jake graduated. She told us that we could *not* have the funeral at the school due to the way he was killed. She said there was a law stating this. At the time, I was mad and didn't understand why this was happening. But I had to move on and take care of Jake. I couldn't stop thinking about what she had said. Jake had given his life for his country, fighting for and defending its people. He wasn't killed in a gunfight on the streets! There are a lot of laws and politics that I do not understand, I guess.

After the runaround with the school, someone contacted us and said their church was large enough to hold around five to six hundred people; they were willing to let us have

Jake's funeral there. There *are* good people around. Now we knew where Jake's funeral services were going to be held, but there was still so much to be done.

The next step was to decide the program for the funeral. The family agreed that there should be music and songs that were important to Jake and the rest of us. There was one song in particular that made an impact in Jake's life. A few weeks before Jake left for Iraq, we had a father-son movie night. During the movie *We Were Soldiers*, a song called "Sgt. MacKenzie" started to play. Jake immediately turned to me and said he wanted that song played at his funeral. All I could say was, "Okay."

There were several other songs played as well. While we were picking the songs out as a family, I could only think about how many times Jake and I had listed to them in the living room, turning the sound up and just relaxing.

The funeral went well. There were a great deal of tears shed, but there were also good times remembered. There were many people there to show their respect. The most amazing sight was to see so many soldiers from Fort Riley paying their respects and remembering a good friend. After the service, Cindy and I stayed behind to say one last good-bye. When the last person left, we opened the casket one last time. I looked at Jake, and tears began to fall. As the casket closed, I turned around and looked at Jake's second family—his army buddies. They were getting ready to take Jake to his final resting place.

As we followed the casket outside, I looked up from the top of the stairs; I was amazed at the sight before my eyes. There were more people lining the streets than I had ever seen before. In that split second, I realized just how many lives Jake had touched. I looked at Cindy, and with tears in my eyes, I told her how much I loved her.

As we drove down Main Street, we watched the people pass by through the windows of the car. I couldn't believe all the children, mothers, fathers, and friends lined up, waving good-bye to a fallen soldier. They were waving the American flag, honoring Jake and his sacrifice. They knew what Jake had given for his country, and they were showing us how much Jake meant to them, even if they didn't know him personally. As we turned off Main Street to the street leading to the cemetery, another amazing sight faced us. All of the children from the Wellsville Elementary School lined the street. Some were crying, some were in awe or stunned, but all were waving the American Flag. After what seemed like an eternity, we arrived at the cemetery. The car doors were opened for us, and all we could do was look around in amazement at how many people were there to pay their respects. I looked at the soldiers' faces that were there; most of them were not showing very much emotion. That is what they are trained to do, but everyone could tell that deep down, they were grieving the loss of one of their own.

As everyone was gathering to listen to the pastor, you could hear a bell ringing. The bell was rung by a man standing at the grave site as everyone was driving in; it was ringing in honor of Jake. After the eulogy, there was a twenty-one gun salute. As "Taps" was played, we all knew that this was the final good-bye to Jake. The military had one last thing to do before lowering Jake into his grave. They folded the American flag that covered Jake's casket. They took a great deal of pride and care in folding that flag. Tears from everyone were flowing as they presented the flag to Cindy. The flag was then placed in its display case where it will stay as long as I live. After the funeral, the family returned home where more people were waiting and kept coming throughout the day.

## Wilson's Funeral Home
### 607 Main Street
### Wellsville, Kansas 66092
### (785) 883-2110

Benji R. Jones

SGT Jacob Lee Butler, age 24 of Wellsville, KS permanently stationed at Ft. Riley, KS died serving his country April 1st, 2003 in As Samawah, Iraq. Funeral services will be held 10AM, Monday, April 14th, 2003 at the Wellsville Baptist Church in Wellsville, KS. Visitation will be from 2-8PM, Sunday, April 13th, 2003 at Wilson's Funeral Home in Wellsville. Military burial services will follow funeral services at the Wellsville Cemetery. Memorial contributions may be made to the Sgt. Jake Butler Trust Fund in care of Wilson's Funeral Home, P.O. Box 486 Wellsville, KS 66092.

Jacob Lee Butler was born April 26, 1978 in Merriam, Kansas the son of James C. and Cynthia D. (Aune) Butler. He lived in Merriam for several years and attended South Park Elementary before moving to Wellsville with his family in 1990. He attended the Wellsville Schools and graduated from Wellsville High School in 1996. After high school Jake worked for Nolkes Cash Saver in Wellsville and for SMH in Olathe before joining the United States Army in November of 1998. He was stationed at Ft. Hood, TX after basic training as a cavalry scout for 2 years. He re-enlisted on March 23, 2001 and was transferred to Ft. Riley, KS. As a cavalry scout, SGT Butler went on tour to Kuwait in 1999 and was later deployed to Kuwait on his second tour in April of 2002 until October of that same year. In January, SGT Butler went to the Mohave Desert in California for 4 weeks for desert training and was then deployed to Kuwait once more on March 2, 2003. SGT Butler advanced into Iraq with his unit, serving in Operation Iraqi Freedom when he gave his life for his country.

Jake was a proud member of the United States Army and a loyal member of the Association of the United States Army. Jake enjoyed hunting, fishing, and raising cattle and loved spending time with his family and friends. He had a great fondness for his two nieces and nephew and will be dearly missed by all that knew him, loved him, and served with him. SGT Butler's awards and decorations include: The Meritorious Service Medal, The Army Commendation Medal with two oak leaf clusters, The Army Achievement Medal, The National Defense Service Medal, The Armed Forces Expeditionary Medal with service star, The Good Conduct Medal, and The Purple Heart, earned in Operation Iraqi Freedom.

Jake is survived by his parents of the home in Wellsville; brother, James C. Butler, Jr. of Wellsville and his son, Jess Horn; brother and his wife, Joshua M. and Chrissy Butler of Ottawa and their two daughters, Shelby and Kaitlyn, his twin brother Joseph D. Butler of Olathe; and brother Justin M. Butler of Wellsville; paternal grandparents, Robert J. and Nancy J. Butler of Baldwin City, KS; 4 aunts, 4 uncles and many cousins. Jake is preceded in death by his maternal grandparents.

# Going through Jake's Things

A few days after the funeral, we received some of Jake's belongings from Iraq. Eli, one of Jake's friends, brought us his duffel bag. It was hard for me to open it and go through his things. I found things that were very important to him, pictures of his nieces and a letter from the family. As I was going through it, I touched everything in it, and it made me feel close to Jake again. I couldn't help but wonder what Jake and his friends had gone through that day.

While going through his things, a memory came rushing back to me. I was taking Jake to Best Buy where we picked up some last-minute things and ended up looking through CDs. I grabbed one and said, "Jake, check this out." It was John Lennon's album called *Imagine*. He said, "Wow!

That's cool." So he took it from me and bought it. Some of the other things we bought that day were some eight-millimeter film and other necessities. I found that film in his duffel bag; I decided to watch it. There was a spot where Jake was filming out of the front window of his truck. As I watched it, I felt as if my love and care for Jake was stronger than ever. While the film was playing, I found tears rolling down my cheeks. The song "Imagine" was playing in the background as the Humvee was bouncing along the dusty road. A sight caught my eye; there, taped to the dash, was a picture of Cindy and me. We had received that picture from the army in Jake's things. Sergeant Corkrean, Jake's platoon sergeant, brought it to us when he came home from Iraq, along with the last letter Jake had written to the family. When he handed us the picture, he told us that when they moved Jake's body away from the Humvee, they had laid the picture with his body.

Thoughts of Jake's death drift in and out of my mind constantly. As I continued to watch the video Jake took in Iraq, I noticed he was heading from Kuwait into Iraq. I suddenly realized I was watching what Jake had done and seen in his last days of his life. As they proceeded, the sun was starting to come up, and you could see the rough terrain and mounds of configured sand dunes and buildings as he passed through the smaller towns. You could see the homes that had been destroyed and cars burning. You could see where the Iraqis had used cars to block the road. When

Jake was filming out the passenger window, there were bodies in the burning vehicles along the road. At one point, there was a body lying in the ditch, covered in a pool of blood. I heard Jake say, "That is disgusting." I wonder what might have been going on in his mind at that moment.

A box James, Jake, and I had put together returned later that month. We took a car radio with two speakers and set it up so Jake could hook up to his Humvee. It took us three or four tries to get it right, but after we finished it, it worked pretty well.

As I continued to watch the tape, Jake's unit went farther into Iraq. They received orders to destroy some heavy Iraqi arms. They came across some heavy gunnery, but there were no Iraqi citizens around. I heard someone tell Jake's unit to put C-4 on the machinery to destroy it and keep it from being used against our military forces in the future. The unit stopped several times to do this. At this time in the film, I saw that everyone in his unit looked tired but seemed to be doing fairly well.

They continued to go farther into Iraq. One day, three of the Humvees got stuck in the mud, and they had to spend a long time getting them out. After they were out, Jake taped himself taking a drink of water and telling us, "Man, I'm tired!" I had to agree with him; he looked tired. The last date on his camcorder was March 29, 2003, which was two days before he died.

# Jake's Last Mission

Jake's day had come; it was April 1, 2003. The mission that he was on was not supposed to happen according to what we were told. It was early morning, and Jake somehow knew in his heart that he would not return alive from that mission. Before he left, he wrote his last letter to his family. When I spoke with Jake's platoon sergeant about the letter, he told me that if he had known what Jake did, he would never have let him go on the mission. I looked at him and said with a chuckle, "Jake would have told you to kiss his ass!" Like he told his mom, "This is what I have been trained for." I knew nothing the sergeant could have said to Jake that day could have changed his mind to complete the mission he had been assigned to carry out. God knew what was to take place that day.

We would soon find out more about the mission they had gone on that day. That morning, Jake and his platoon went through a checkpoint. As they went through, the soldiers waved and told them to have a good day. However, what they failed to tell them as they passed would soon prove to carry heavy consequences. The day before, about five miles ahead on the same road Jake and his platoon were on, some heavy body-armored Bradleys had taken heavy gunfire. This happened at the intersection of one of the main roads that goes through As Samawah, Iraq, on a bridge called the Pipeline Bridge. The area had already been taken over by the military, and they knew what was there. It was a simple bridge with a pipeline running parallel with it. They were sent out tin cans or Humvees. The Humvee is different from a Bradley because it doesn't have body armor. That day, the Humvee Jake was in took fourteen shots to the passenger side, where he was sitting.

Jake was wingman to his section sergeant, SSgt. V. As the platoon reached the area they were supposed to check out, all the Humvees were headed north. Jake's Humvee was seventy-five feet west of the Pipeline Bridge and approximately fifty feet away from SSgt. V., running parallel with each other. The third Humvee in the group was Jake's platoon sergeant, SSgt. C., which was one hundred feet south of the first two Humvees. SSgt. V.'s gunner looked to the east across the Euphrates River and reported a truck with men in the back with RPGs. SSgt. V. radioed back to ask permission to fire but was told to stand down. He requested a second time for permission to fire and received the same answer, to stand down. Before he could ask the third time, an RPG hit his Humvee two feet in front of the engine compartment. When it hit, it caused the driver to be knocked out of the vehicle and injured SSgt. V. and his gunner. After the RPG struck, Jake ordered his driver to "get the guys and get the f*** out of here!" These were his last words.

As Jake's truck backed up and turned around to block SSgt. V.'s Humvee, about twenty-five to forty Iraqi soldiers came running from behind a fence along the ditch on the southwest corner of the intersection toward Jake's Humvee. As his driver pulled up next to SSgt. V.'s Humvee, Jake's truck took fourteen shots to the passenger side; one bullet hit Jake in the head, and three hit Jake's gunner. As the young men were taking fire, SSgt. C. ran from the last Humvee across the line of fire and toward SSgt. V.'s truck, grabbing the injured gunner and helping him to the hood of the third Humvee. SSgt. V. was on the radio asking for help; they needed air support. They also needed to destroy his Humvee that was struck so the Iraqi soldiers would not be able to use any of it.

When the gunfire ended, everyone in Jake's platoon regrouped and returned to the checkpoint where they could check on Jake. No one knew how bad Jake was hit. As they pulled his door open, Jake slumped forward, and blood ran down his face. The men pulled Jake out of the truck in his blood-soaked uniform and tried to revive him. They didn't know it was too late. They didn't know that Jake had been shot in the head and that he was already gone. The gunshot wound proved to be fatal, and Jake had died instantly. After they had done everything they could do for him, they laid his body on the porch of one of the houses they were using for an aid station. They covered him with a sheet, took the picture Jake had with him (a picture of his mother and me), and laid it on his body.

In the time of war, the rules of engagement should be shoot first and ask questions later. For some reason, the day Jake was killed, the rules were "Do *not* fire unless fired upon." Jake's body would lie on the porch of this house until the next morning. After Jake's buddies came home from Iraq, Sergeant C. told me that one of the hardest things he has ever had to do happened the day Jake was killed. He and another soldier had to clean Jake's blood from the Humvee. The injured gunner was sent to Germany and then to Washington for recovery then finally to Texas for his injuries that he sustained that day. He was discharged from the army because he could no longer do his job; after all, he had already given *so much* for his country.

DEPARTMENT OF THE ARMY
Headquarters, 1st Battalion, 41st Infantry Regiment
3rd Brigade, 1st Armored Division
Fort Riley, Kansas 66442

6 April 2003

Office of the Commander

Mr. and Mrs. James Butler
28 East 2300 Road
Wellsville, KS  66092

Dear Mr. and Mrs. Butler:

The soldiers of my command join me in extending to you our deepest sympathy on the death of your son in combat, Sergeant Jacob Butler. He was a special soldier to all of my command. He was always in front of my combat formations, using his keen mind, great scouting skills, and mission focus to keep us safe. He died performing those duties. Three days later the information he gained, for my mechanized infantry battalion, caused us to successfully attack a heavily defended bridge to cross the Euphrates River and liberate three Iraqi cities.

We know the irreparable loss that you have suffered and fully realize there is little we can say to help you in this moment of sorrow. I was at the battalion medical aid station where he was evacuated to, by his fellow soldiers, and pronounced dead. I spoke to the treating physician and saw Jacob. I can assure you that Jacob died instantly and did not suffer.

Your son carried a picture of you both with him in a lovely frame. Outside the medical aid station where Jacob laid it was a beautiful day. The sun was bright, it was cool, and there were lovely palm trees that lined the Euphrates River. Jacob's scout section, his platoon sergeant and myself placed the picture of you above him, prayed for him, your family, and asked him to continue to watch over us from heaven as he did on earth. In time, you may find personal reassurance in the thought that he died in the service of his country and that our gratitude as a command, as an Army, and as a nation are deep and lasting. We will not forget him. He will be an everlasting memory to this unit's history.

Our heartfelt condolences are extended to you and the members of your family in your bereavement.

Sincerely,

GEORGE GECZY III
Lieutenant Colonel, United States Army
Commanding

# In the Aftermath of the Loss

From the day we were told about Jake's death until the time his body arrived back in the United States, there were several ceremonies we were asked to attend as a family. One of them was held at Fort Riley. I remember standing back from the stage a little and looking at where the boots were sitting, one with the gun barrel aimed down toward the ground with a helmet hung on the end. Just this sight made the pain all too real; it was just overwhelming to think that Jake truly was not coming home at the end of the ceremonies. General Hemlock was the head of all the ceremonies, and one day he made a great suggestion to me. He thought it might be a good idea to send a box of Jake's personal belongings to Iraq and bury it close to where Jake had been killed. I wasn't sure if what he was saying to me would be feasible, but he reassured me that it would because Jake's platoon was still in Iraq. He told me the reason he felt it was a good thing to do was because it would give Jake's platoon a chance to be a part of the good-bye to Jake.

I agreed to do it, and the family began to get some things together that meant a lot to them and also to Jake. Everyone added something, from pictures to other personal items. The grandchildren, Jake's nieces and nephew, even put in a teddy bear. I had a watch that always hung from by belt loop; it was given to me by Shelby and KK for Father's Day one year. I put it in the box with the time set to Kansas time.

When the box arrived in Iraq, Jake's platoon could not bury it where they had planned because of all the looting going on around the Pipeline Bridge. They were afraid that if they went ahead as planned, the box would be stolen. So instead of burying it, they decided to place it in the river. The platoon was able to find a waterproof box, and they wrapped the box in plastic. They then stopped all the traffic on the bridge and drove a single Hummer on to it; with a few last words in memory of Jake, they threw the box into the Euphrates River.

Back at home, calls were still coming in about Jake's death. About three days after we were told Jake had been killed, Senator Sam Brownback came to the house. It was a big surprise to the whole family to have a senator coming to our house. We knew he was visiting us out of respect for Jake and our entire family. While the senator was at the house, he asked Cindy and me if there was anything he could do for us. I told him that there was something he could do for me. I then told him about the promise I had made to Jake about going to Iraq if he didn't make it back. Sam told me that he couldn't really see a problem with me going, and he would see what he could do. I then told him I had one other request. I told him that it would be really great for the family if we could all meet the president, Sam again agreed that he didn't see a problem with that and would see what he could do. After that, we all talked with the senator for a couple of hours, and upon leaving, he turned and said that he would be in touch.

A few months later, our town had what we call Wellsville Days. A few days before the big event, the military got in touch with us and told us that Jake would be receiving one more medal, the Silver Star. They told us they were planning on presenting the medal to Cindy and me during the Wellsville Days parade. Then the town of Wellsville asked us if we would be the grand marshals, and of course we told them we would be honored.

Finally the day of the parade came. Since we were the grand marshals, we got to ride in a car in the parade. During the parade, the car stopped in front of the large stage that was set up for the evening events. Josh Elmer, the man who was driving the car, got out and opened the doors for us, and we proceeded toward the stage. Once I got to the top of the stairs, I was faced with a surprise. There stood Colonel Geczy, Jake's colonel. Colonel Geczy looked at the people gathered around and told them how proud he was of Jake and what he had done the day he was killed. He told everyone that if it had not been for what Jake did that day, many more lives would have been lost. After his brief announcement, he presented Cindy and me with the Silver Star for Jake's heroic action on that day. This time, Jake's platoon was able to attend, and they all stood so tall and proud on Main Street. Looking at them, I couldn't help but think about how proud Jake would have been of his buddies. Jake would have also been proud of the citizens of Wellsville for everything they had done to support his family and all the troops throughout the world.

# A Promise Kept

All through the pain and sadness of Jake's loss, the army had been good to my family. Because of that, I decided to ask them to help me fulfill my promise to Jake of going to Iraq. It seemed like no matter who I talked to, I received the same response: "It's just too dangerous." No matter how many times I heard it, I always had the same thing to say in return: "You think I don't know how dangerous it is in Iraq? For God's sake, my son lost his life there." I knew at this time that I was not going to get help from anyone, so I began the process by myself. I first applied for my passport then went through all the shots and medical tests I would need to go overseas. During the application for my visa, while doing this I was asked why I was going to Kuwait. I just said that I was traveling through Kuwait to get into Iraq so I could see where my son gave his life for his country. Within seven days, I had received my Kuwait visa. Then I decided to write one last letter for help, this one to the president. My letter is as follows:

Dear President Bush,

As I sit here on this twentieth day of April, nineteen days after our son Sgt. Jacob L. Butler gave his life for peace and freedom for our country and others, I look at one wall in our house. This wall is filled with all of his certificates of achievement and a few of his last medals, the Purple Heart and the Bronze Star.

Jake, as we called him at home, and I were not only father and son but very good friends. We were the kind of friends that could talk about anything. Jake loved his country, freedom, and the simple things in life. That is what he wanted for other people in the world.

Jake went farther in his almost twenty-five years than I have in my forty-seven years. The family—Cindy (his mother), and his brothers James Jr., Josh, Joe, and Justin—would stand behind and support Jake in whatever he wanted to do. Jake in return would stand behind his brothers in whatever they chose to do. I'm not a very good speller or writer, but I just wanted to say thanks. The whole family and I would like to say thank you for all you have done for us and Jake. He will be missed but not forgotten in our hearts.

Senator Sam Brownback stopped by one day and talked with Cindy and me, and I asked him about one last request I had, and I hope you might understand, being that you are a father as well. Joe, Jake's twin brother, and I would like to go to Iraq and stand where Jake gave his life at the bridge near As Samawah.

The platoon he was with is coming home around the first part of June, but I would like to go before they come home so they might go with us to pay respects to Jake.

I know things might still be rough and dangerous, but every day of our lives is like that now that Jake is gone. That is why we have God in our lives.

I hope that you will consider my request as a father. I hope to hear from you soon so that I may be able to finish laying Jake to rest.

May God be with you and your family.

James Butler
Father of Sgt. Jacob L. Butler

By the time I wrote this letter, I had heard through the grapevine that some military and government personnel were calling me a disgruntled and possibly crazy parent. They just did not understand that I started to deal with his death a couple of months before Jake died because of what I had seen in my dream.

What I found out through my experience is that if you are in politics or have money, you can do just about anything, but if you have a son or a daughter that has given their life for their country, you can hardly do anything. I never did hear back from the president, but I do hope he may have read my letter. I did, however, hear from Sam Brownback, who wanted to know how everything was going. Through all of the letters and contacts, I came to realize why most of the people I was asking for help would not put their necks on the line for me. It was because if anything happened to me while in Iraq, it would probably mean the end of their career.

I finally got things squared away to the best of my abilities and started to prepare to go to Iraq. However, on October 1, Cindy and I received a letter from Senator Pat Roberts's office. The letter was exactly like all the others we had gotten from the government and military. They told us what we already had heard several times, that it was too dangerous to go to Iraq. It just reminded me of what I knew from the beginning; if I was to go to Iraq, I would have to do it on my own.

As I read the letter from the senator's office, I remembered the conversation I had with Colonel Geczy the day Cindy and I got Jake's Silver Star. The colonel had told me I would never make it across the border from Kuwait to Iraq. I remember telling him that once I left the United States, I knew about all the risks, from mines to being kidnapped. I was on my own with no expectations of help from anyone.

I didn't know if I would return from Iraq, so the night before I left, I took the family out to dinner: Cindy, James Jr., Josh, Joe, Justin, Chrissy, Shelby, KK, Jess, my mom and dad, my brother Rob, and Sara, Jake's friend. We went to one of Jake's favorite places, Chili's. We all enjoyed ourselves and had a good time. As we were leaving, Sara gave me a letter. She said if something happened and that I didn't come back, I had to be sure to say hi to Jake for her. I smiled at her and said I would. When I got home that night, I didn't sleep much like always since there was a lot going on in my mind.

After Cindy and I returned home that night from dinner, I thought about all of the boys and my wish of growing up with them had come true. I was their father, but sometimes I felt like a brother because we had done so many things together. I was right beside them all the time as they grew into young men, and then they started down their own road of life, but they still included their mom and me in it.

The day my flight would leave for Iraq, October 10, had come. Cindy, Chrissy, and the grandchildren helped me finish up the last of my packing. I walked into the room addition, which is now called Jake's room. I looked at all of Jake's things and thought about how proud I was of him and how much I missed him. I knew where I was going, and I knew deep down that I was going to keep my promise to Jake. I started wondering what life would have been like if Jake had not been killed compared to how it is now, but I soon realized there was no sense in wondering. Now I would leave the United States, and I have so many things ahead of me that I have never faced before. This will be the first time I have left the country, the first time I have even flown on a plane, but these are small things compared to fulfilling the last promise made to my son.

As the family and I started to walk through the house and past Jake's wall, Cindy and I stopped and looked at the accomplishments our son had made. I turned to Cindy and looked at her, hugged her, and told her how much I loved her. I knew she was having trouble with the idea of me leaving because tears started rolling down her face. As she wiped them away, she looked at me and said, "I hope you find what you're looking for." In that moment, I knew that she understood what I needed to do, and I smiled.

When we arrived at the airport, all of the family gathered around the car to help me get all of my things unloaded. As we started toward the entrance, KK asked me to carry her, so I picked her up and put her on my shoulders. KK pointed up to the sky and said, "Grandpa, look" as a jet flew over our heads. Even though she didn't know exactly what was going on, KK was able to keep the tension low by just one simple remark.

We then proceeded to the terminal where a news reporter from the *Kansas City Star* had come to see me off. She started to ask me a few questions and then asked me if I would allow her to fly with me to Chicago. I looked at her and jokingly remarked, "What, you don't want to fly with me to Iraq?" She said she would love to go with me, but the *Kansas City Star* would not let her because they would have no protection. I then told her that I had all the protection I would ever need—my son.

When it was time for me to go through the security gates and leave the family, I turned to them and said my good-byes. Joe was having the most difficult time with my leaving, so I gave him a hug. He then looked at me and, while wiping the tears from his face, begged me not to go. With tears streaming down my face, I told him that I had made a promise to Jake and that he knew I had to go. I told them all not to worry, that I would be home soon. I knew this was hard for everyone because they had just lost their brother and were worried that they could lose me too. I finally got to Chrissy and gave her a hug. She whispered to me that Josh really didn't want me to go through with this. I hugged her a little tighter and said, "I know, but deep down they all know I have to do what I must. They may not agree, but they will support what I have to do."

After I went through security, the reporter and I loaded on the jet. As we began our ascent, all I could think about was the promise that I had made to Jake and how much I loved the family. I knew that I had a date to keep, October 14, and I knew no matter what it took, I was going to keep that date. As I sat on the jet that day, there were so many things going through my mind, like the call I received earlier that day from someone that had tried to help me get into Iraq. He told me that I should really change my plans, that I shouldn't go to Iraq because it wasn't safe. I told him, "You think I don't know that? My son lost his life there, and besides, there is someone much higher than us, and my life has already been laid out for me, so whatever the outcome, it was meant to be." As we started flying up through the clouds, I looked out of the jet window and thought about how soft the clouds looked.

As the flight continued, I started thinking about the dreams that I had and about something that had happened to me when I was in the sixth grade. My teacher had just come back from the Middle East, and she told us how old and beautiful everything was. She had gone to the Middle East just before the seven-day war. It seemed kind of strange as the class had gathered around her desk to look at the pictures she had taken and the other things she brought back. She looked at me and told me I would go to the Middle East someday. I never thought that something told to me in the sixth grade would end up coming true.

I knew this trip to Iraq would probably change my life and that I may not be the same person I was when I left. As I was flying to Chicago, I was thinking about how many smart people there are in the world but how sometimes they seem to lack common sense. People that were around me after Jake was killed knew I was not the same person. I really was a different man, but I still carried the same morals. The whole family has changed in some way or another. I remember as I was getting ready to fly from Kansas City to Chicago, before I got on the jet, I had given Cindy one last hug and kiss as she looked at me with her tear-filled eyes, and I told her I loved her. I knew if anything happened to me, she would keep the family together.

When I got to O'Hare International Airport in Chicago, I made a phone call to Kuwait City to reserve a motel room for two nights. I had several phone numbers of people that would help me in any way. One of the numbers was for the proper paperwork to get me across the Kuwait-Iraqi border, and another number was for anything I might need for protection to travel through Iraq.

At the O'Hare airport, I had a four-hour layover. The reporter asked me if I wanted to eat; she smiled at me and told me she was buying. After we were done, I went outside the terminal, and as we were talking, she said she was worried about me. I told her I would be fine. Then she asked me something I will never forget. As she was standing there, she looked as if she were looking for the right words and then asked, "When you get to where Jake was killed, are you going to kill yourself?"

I just looked at her with what I can imagine to be a very blank gaze and asked her if she thought I was crazy. I told her this trip wasn't about that. "I guess you and many others don't understand anything about the love I have for my son and the last promise I made to him. It is a promise as a father I have to keep. I made my peace with God a long time ago, and I don't fear the fact of dying."

Then she told me that her bosses had asked her to ask me. I thought to myself, *I guess if I was out to take my own life, they would have had one hell of a story.* As it was getting close for me to leave, she told me she was going to try to get to Iraq while I was there.

Finally it was time for me to catch my plane, but it was all the way on the other side of the airport, which I thought was crazy. I flew from O'Hare to Amsterdam then boarded another plane to Kuwait City. As the plane was coming into Kuwait City, it circled several times before the plane dropped through the clouds. The moon had come up; it was full and bright and looked so beautiful. The plane continued to drop below the clouds, and I could finally see Kuwait City. It was lit up just like a Christmas tree; the streets had lights down the entire block, and it seemed so beautiful for something man had made.

The plane landed on the runway and approached the terminal to unload. Everyone seemed to be in such a rush, so I just waited for it to clear. As I walked into the terminal, I found myself in a different world. A world where I didn't look or dress like anyone else, and I couldn't even speak the same language. They did have some signs in English that I could read, so I found my way to Customs, which turned out to be a small room with one desk and Kuwait soldiers all around the outside. As I approached one of the soldiers and showed him my passport and visa, he told me to sit down outside of the little office, so I did. After about one hour, he came back and gave me my passport, which had been stamped.

After going through another metal detector, I found myself going down a wide walkway with people all around me with yellow ropes on both sides of the walkway. I turned and looked to my right and saw a beautiful young American woman holding a sign that said Mr. Butler. I thought, *Wait a minute, no one knew I was coming*. I didn't know whether to go up to her or to keep walking, but I decided I didn't have anything to lose, so I walked toward her, and she said, "Mr. Butler?" I said yes. She then told me, "Would you come with me?"

As we walked around the yellow ropes, she said, "I would like for you to stand with these three gentlemen while I go and find the others that are looking for you." I stood with the three gentlemen for a while, then they finally introduced themselves as the United States military. I still didn't know what to think because they were not in uniform. After a few minutes had gone by, the woman came back. From there we headed for the parking lot, and they all started discussing who I was going to go with. After a few minutes, she won; I was going with her and not the other soldiers. I found out later that the other soldiers had orders from a colonel to escort me back to the United States.

We left the airport and drove to the Dohah base outside of Kuwait City. We drove onto the base and went through several guard stations. It was close to midnight, and there wasn't any wind blowing. I stepped out of the vehicle, and the smell of sewage that hit me was very strong. I looked at the traffic that was moving around the base and then realized there were four soldiers asking me to come with them. We walked through huge concrete barricades that surrounded the barracks. As we walked to one of the doors, one of the soldiers unlocked the door, and we went in. The soldier handed me the key and told me a colonel would be by in a few minutes to talk with me. I said okay. After about fifteen minutes had passed by, there was a knock at the door, so I answered the door, and the man at the door introduced himself as did I. After the introductions, he looked at me and told me he didn't know how I made it as far as I had. I looked him straight in the eye and told him there was a much bigger and higher power than the military or government at work here. He smiled at me and told me that he didn't know that I was coming until ten minutes before the plane had landed. Then after a minute of silence, he asked me why I was in Iraq.

So I began to tell him about the promise that I had made to Jake and how he was killed in As Samawah on April 1, 2003. After we were done talking, the colonel told me he didn't know if he could help me, but he would see what he could do. I told him that I appreciated everything he could do, but if he couldn't help, it didn't matter because I had a date to keep. I was going to be where Jake had lost his life. The Colonel smiled at me and asked me if I would meet with the general tomorrow and tell him my story. As the colonel was walking out the door, he asked me if I had called my wife since I had gotten to Kuwait. I told him I hadn't, and he showed me the phone in the barrack. I called Cindy and let her know that I was doing well and told her to tell everyone that I loved them.

It was now October 11 at about 6:15 a.m., and a major was at the door. As the major and I walked down the street to the chow hall, I watched all the young men and women that were stationed at Dohah. I thought about Jake and how many times he had been there. We walked a little farther and went into the chow hall; it was like a buffet. There were hundreds of soldiers in and out. After the major and I got our food, we sat down and started eating, and about halfway through our meal, the colonel came in. He walked up to the major and me, and he had a strange look on his face. He then told the major and me that he had gotten a phone call from a newspaper reporter from the *Kansas City Star*. He said that she said that if the military didn't stop detaining Mr. Butler and holding him against his will, she would print how the military was treating him. The colonel then asked me what I had said to my wife when I called her because he thought that I had accidentally said something that started this story.

The major and I finished eating, and I went back to my quarters to call Cindy to see if the reporter had called her and to ask what she had said to her. After calling Cindy, I found out that the reporter wasn't saying what Cindy had told her. I then told Cindy to call her and tell her I was fine and wasn't being detained and that the military was taking care of me and trying to help me keep my promise that I had made to Jake.

Later that morning, the colonel came to my quarters and asked me if I knew a Mike Webb, and I told him, "Yes, I know him as Chief Elf." He wanted to try to help me keep my promise to Jake. He then asked me if anyone had paid for my plane ticket or anything to get me to Iraq, and I told him no and asked why. He said that Mr. Webb was trying to say the military was trying to keep me from doing what I came to do. The colonel then asked me to contact Mr. Webb and tell him what was going on.

After the colonel left, I called Mr. Webb. As we talked, he told me I owed the reporter a story for the *Kansas City Star*. I told him I didn't owe anybody anything but Jake, and that was why I was in Iraq. I told him that if people kept saying that the military was detaining me, it's just going to make it harder for me to keep the promise to Jake. I told him I was fine and didn't need any help. After I got off the phone, I told the colonel that I didn't think we would have any more problems with the *Kansas City Star* or Mr. Webb. When I was talking to the colonel, he didn't know where this reporter had gotten information stating that I was being detained. I shook my head and said I didn't either.

Now it was early afternoon, and the colonel came to my quarters to get me so I could go talk with the general. I had to go through several security points to get to the general. As I walked into a building and up the stairs to a room, the colonel asked me to have a seat. After a few minutes, he came back and took me to the general's office. I went in and sat down, and after a few minutes, the general came in and introduced himself to me and asked me if I would tell him my story. So I began to tell him. After about an hour had passed and I was finished telling my story, the general looked at me and smiled, and then he told me what the colonel and he had done. He said that they had contacted another general, and the general told them, "If Mr. Butler is as true of an American as you say he is, then you do whatever it takes to get him to where his son had given his life and get him back out."

As I got up out of my chair and shook the general's hand and looked into his eyes, I knew that he understood me from a father's point of view.

After the colonel and I left the general's office, we started walking down the road, and the colonel told me that he probably wouldn't talk to me much over the next twenty-four hours because he needed that much time to get things ready to help me keep my date of October 14. As he left my quarters, I shook his hand and said thank you.

Later on that night, a major and the lady that picked me up from the airport came to my quarters and took me out for dinner in Kuwait City. As we were driving to the city, I looked at the traffic. It was nuts; the people drove like they were crazy. On the way to Kuwait City, we were driving down the highway, and I don't think anyone was driving under 100 miles per hour. There were people stopped in the middle of the highway, and there were people standing by their cars and talking. We finally got to the restaurant safely. I got something to eat, and I had this Kuwait money, so I bought them dinner, mainly because I did not want to bring that money home. We then drove back to the base, and they dropped me off at my quarters around 10:30 p.m. The colonel came by around 11:00 p.m. to tell me what he had found out and to brief me about what was going to happen. As we were talking, he showed me an aerial map of where Jake was killed. As he finished telling me what he had found out, he then told me that he was going to put this mission together as a combat mission, and he would be back tomorrow in the evening to let me know more about it.

It was about 3:00 a.m. on October 11. I walked outside of my quarters, and as I looked at the sky and the moon, I felt so peaceful, but it was short lived because I saw that the soldiers were still moving up and down the streets in Dohah.

It was around 7:30 a.m. when the major came by to take me to breakfast. After we were finished, I returned to my quarters. The day seemed like it was going really slow, so I walked down to the PX, which is a retail store on the base for military use only, where I bought several things for the family. While I was by the PX, I got something to eat. I couldn't believe they had a KFC on base. I returned to my quarters and watched the news on the TV. From what the news was telling everyone, it sounded worse than what it seemed to be, but of course, I wasn't in Baghdad.

All I could think about the rest of the afternoon was Jake and the family and how much I loved all of them. I looked at the picture of Shelby, KK, and Jess, and I remembered how much Jake loved them and how the family loved Jake. We will never forget him, but our love and support for each other needed to go on because Jake would want us all to stand together and to stand strong. I knew that the promise I had made to Jake would be fulfilled with the help of Colonel Snow.

It was around 10:00 p.m. when the colonel came to my quarters. As he started talking, he asked me if instead of being where Jake was killed on October 14, did I have a problem being there on October 13. I looked at him and asked him why. He told me, "If it gets out to the media, it would be like a zoo." I told him I wouldn't have a problem with that. He asked me if something happened and that the media did show up on October 13, what would I have wanted to do. I told him if that did indeed happen, we would just have to call everything off. I told him that I would then have to go another day. The colonel looked at me and smiled and said, "That's all I wanted to hear."

Colonel then began briefing me; he told me he was going to order some soldiers to help with this mission, but it ended up that he didn't have to because all the soldiers that were needed volunteered. Hearing that sent chills down my back. He then told me on October 13, 2003, at 7:00 a.m. that the soldier with him would pick me up in front of my quarters. We had finished going over everything, and the colonel told me he would see me in the morning and told me to get some sleep. I told the colonel thanks for everything and that my family and I really appreciated it. I shook his hand, and he walked out the door.

When I was in Kuwait, I didn't sleep much. All I could keep thinking about was the promise I made to Jake, the family, and what is was like being here where Jake had lost his life. It was about midnight, so I went outside to look around. The sky was still clear and the moon was bright, just like the night before. Again I remember it being very peaceful.

As I stood outside thinking about the next day, a soldier, who was standing by the street, and I began talking. He asked me why I was in Kuwait, and I told him about the promise I made to Jake. I asked him if he was going home, and he told me that he was getting ready to go back to Baghdad. He told me that he was going back to help finish up the fighting. He had been away from it all because he had been injured. After talking for a while, he told me how proud he was of Jake and what he had done and how sorry he was for our loss. I smiled at him and told him to be safe out there and come home soon. He said thanks, and a vehicle pulled up, and he climbed in and left.

It was now 6:00 a.m. on October 13. I knew that this day would not only be a big day in my life, but what I hoped to take back and show the family would be very memorable to them because they might be able to get a glimpse of what Jake had seen in his last few minutes of life. As I got ready, I put on a pair of Jake's combat boots; it was strange that Jake and I were almost the same size in shoes. As I put the boots on, there was a knock at the door. I opened it, and there was the colonel. He asked me if I was ready, and I just smiled at him and said, "Yes, are you?" He told me as we walked to the vehicle not to worry about anything; his men were all focused on the mission. When we got to the vehicle that was taking me to the tarmac, the colonel handed me a bulletproof vest and helped me put it on. I would say it weighed around thirty pounds or so, and then they gave me a military helmet to put on. We drove down the street a couple of city blocks, and as I got out, I saw three Black Hawk helicopters sitting across from me. There was one soldier that was assigned to stay as close as he could to me and take care of me; I guess you could say that he was my bodyguard.

As I loaded into the Black Hawk, I was told not to put anything I was carrying under my seat. I was seated on the passenger side by a back window. As we were getting ready to lift off, I thought to myself I never flew on a plane, and now I was in a helicopter. The colonel handed me a set of headphones so I would be able to hear what was going on and told me that if I needed anything, I could push the microphone and talk to him. As we lifted off, I couldn't believe how loud it was inside the Black Hawk; there was no air moving where I was sitting, and it was hot.

As we flew over the Kuwaiti and Iraqi border, the colonel pointed it out to me. I looked out of the window and could see the rough terrain. I thought about what Jake and the others might have been thinking about that night as they crossed that area. We flew a little farther, and the ground began to look so flat and open. It wasn't like home where we had grass; it was all desert. By now we were probably about two hundred feet or less in the air as we flew over what I would call sheet tent, and all the Iraqi people came out and waved at us.

After about one hour into our flight, the colonel pointed out an air base out in the middle of nowhere; he called this airbase Taleto. I remember this air base from Jake's letter because in his letter, he told his mom and me that they were getting ready to take it over. We landed on the tarmac, and everyone got out of the Black Hawks. They began to refuel them, which took about ten to fifteen minutes, then we crossed the tarmac once more and reloaded. The first Black Hawk lifted off, and the hawk I was in followed. As we flew closer to As Samawah, there were raised fields with water around them. I guess this is where they raised their crops, but I figured they must have had some way to pump their water from the Euphrates River or the Tigris River. When we began to fly over As Samawah, I could see that everything looked so green from above; we had to wait until the soldiers on the ground gave us a signal that it was all right for us to land. After we were on the ground, we would not have radio contact for around one to one and a half hours, so Colonel Snow needed to make sure everything was going to go as well as could be expected.

As we landed and were getting out of the Black Hawk, rocks were blowing off the ground, and we ran to find ground cover as the rest of the soldiers arrived. After everyone was on the ground, we started to walk down a path toward town. There were Iraqi people all around, and as we were walking, the people from As Samawah were coming up to us, talking in a language that I could not understand. After about a mile, we came to one of the main streets that ran through As Samawah. We crossed the road to a sidewalk that ran along the Euphrates River and turned south along the main street. There were people all around. As we walked south, we crossed the area where Jake's sergeant's Humvee was hit with a rocket-propelled grenade. You could still see the burn marks on the pavement. As I walked through this area, I felt something of Jake's presence. We walked about another one hundred yards, and the colonel asked me if this area would be all right. I nodded my head yes. I walked to the Euphrates River and looked out over the river; it seemed so wide, and it looked as smooth as glass.

The colonel had brought the radio with him, and he sat it on the ground behind a power pole. The reason that he brought the radio was so I might be able to play the CD that Jake's mother and I had played at his funeral and another CD he and I had picked up before he left to go to Iraq. The first CD the colonel put in the player contained a song that Jake had asked me to play at his funeral about two months before he left for Iraq. Jake and I were watching a movie called *We Were Soldiers*, and the song was "Sgt. MacKenzie." The other songs—"I Believe," "Only Time," "Darlin' Be Home Soon," and "Proud to Be an American"—were also on the CD. When I was listening to these songs, it reminded me of the times Jake and I listened to them or as Cindy and I played them when he was gone overseas.

The CD player was playing the songs loud as I stood along the river. I looked around at the soldiers that surrounded me, and I couldn't help but think how proud Jake would have been of each and every one of them for helping me to fulfill the promise that I had made to him. Colonel Snow came up to me and asked me if I was doing all right and handed me another bottle of water. I told him that everything was okay. Colonel Snow then bent down and placed the second CD into the radio. This CD was one that Jake and I had bought just before he went to Iraq. As the song "Imagine" began to play, I started thinking of the film that Jake had recorded a few days before he was killed. On the tape, he was filming through the front windshield of his Humvee, and as he was filming, the song "Imagine" was playing, and mounted on his dash was a picture of his mom and me. This song and the others brought tears to my eyes.

After the last song had played, I told the colonel I would like to throw the last CD into the Euphrates River. He said, "Okay," and we set out to find a good launch pad. We got closer to a point that extended out toward the river, and as I stood there ready to throw the CD out into the river, I thought to myself, *This one is for you, Jake.* As the CD hit the river, it came out of its case. I watched as the CD sank and the case kept floating. To me this was kind of ironic, like the CD symbolized Jake as being gone from the earth, but the case stayed on the surface, symbolizing he will always be with us in spirit. It was a good release of all my energy that had been building up inside since I heard of Jake's death.

When I was there and the songs were playing, I felt how much I was going to miss Jake, but like he said in his last letter he sent home to us, "Don't forget me," and I can say with all honesty in my heart that I know I will never forget him.

After we were finished, all the soldiers gathered around, and we all started walking back to the landing site. When we were walking down the main street, the people from As Samawah were walking beside us and talking to one of the soldiers that was with us. The children were smiling and waving, and I thought about how Jake helped give these people in As Samawah peace and freedom.

As we got back to the landing site, we had to wait for about fifteen minutes before the Black Hawk would pick us up. I started talking to my bodyguard, and he asked me if I felt like a soldier. I looked at him and said, "If you give me that M-16, I would." He looked at me and laughed. I looked toward the sky. I could see the Black Hawk coming back. We then loaded the helicopters and headed back for Dohah. When we flew over the Euphrates River and the spot where Jake was killed, I remembered in one of Jake's letters he said we'd all be together soon, and you know what? He was right.

When we were about fifteen minutes from landing, I started to feel sick. It was over one hundred degrees in the back of the Black Hawk, and there was no air moving. I looked at the colonel and put my hand over my mouth. The soldier across from me knew what I needed, and he passed me a plastic bag, and I filled it up. We landed and got onto the tarmac, and I gave the colonel the plastic bag and told him he could have his water back. He looked at me and grinned then whispered, "I won't tell anyone." I then told him he didn't need to worry about it; I would end up telling others. After all, I was only human. I then asked him if he would have all the soldiers gather around. When they were all gathered, I told them Jake would have been so proud of all of them for helping me, and my family and I deeply appreciated what they had all done. After talking to all of them, I shook each and every one of their hands.

After the colonel had debriefed them, he asked me what I was going to do next. I told him I had kept my promise to Jake, and now I had to get home to my family. He then told me he would like to come by my home sometime when he was in Fort Leavenworth, after he returned home from Iraq. I told him my door was always open and that I think my family and Cindy would love to meet him.

The time had come for me to fly back to the United States. I called Cindy to let her know when my flight was coming in so she could pick me up at the airport. I would be getting back into Kansas around eleven in the evening on October 16.

As I got off the plane, Cindy and a couple of the boys as well as my grandson Jess met me. I was very happy to see them all. After we got all my things together and were loaded in the car, they asked if I wanted to go eat. I said, "Yeah, and I would also like something to drink," and they all laughed.

# Life Goes On

The things that have happened in our life since Jake was killed have been hard to deal with, but our family continues to stand strong and put our trust in God. We will make it, and I will always know that Jake and I will be together soon.

Shortly after returning home, I received a call from Colonel G. He told me that the army was going to dedicate a shooting range outside Baghdad to Jake. It would be called the Butler Range Complex. Cindy and I knew Jake would be honored to have a shooting range named after him. The entire family was proud of this.

Before Jake left for Iraq, he was dating Sara. They actually broke it off months before but remained friends. Jake told me that while in the army, he didn't want to be married because you're already married to the army. After he left the army, he wanted to marry Sara. Even though

Jake and Sara were technically over, they continued to write back and forth while he was in Iraq.

Sara went on to marry a good friend of Jake's in the army. They now have two beautiful children. He was kind enough to ask my permission before dating Sara. He knew that she was still close to our family and didn't want to offend or hurt us. I told him it was time to get on with his life, and although Jake was never coming home, he wouldn't mind. He was in a better place.

The family has gone through so much since Jake's death. The words of "Don't forget me" run through my head no matter where I'm at or what I'm doing. One of Jake's army friends told me that while with Jake, all he talked about was how much he loved his family. This young soldier told me that he didn't have as much love for his family as Jake did for his.

In August 2003, everyone that was with Jake on the day of his death came to our home for a party. We knew some of them while others we did not. Jake spoke of several of his fellow soldiers in letters, so we felt like we already knew them. Thirty-one soldiers showed up that day.

Some of the soldiers wanted to talk about what happened that day while others did not. We were glad that they told us what really happened that day because it gave us a better understanding of what really happened. The soldiers that wished to not participate simply left the conversation. Cindy and I really didn't expect for them to talk about what happened when they came. We wanted them to enjoy themselves and relax for the day.

I asked the soldiers to come to the front of the house where we had poles with yellow and black ribbons tied around them. I asked them to please help me remove them. As we stood, we tried not to cry. For some of us it was too much.

After the ribbon cutting, Cindy and I took all the soldiers to Jake's grave. We stood around with a beer in our hands. One beer was placed on his grave site, and with a laugh and a smile, we said, "This one's for you." I walked up to the grave site with the grandkids, opened the beer, took a swig, and poured the rest on Jake's grave. After about thirty minutes of visiting, we all left.

After almost nine years of struggling with the loss of Jake and what happened on April 1, 2003, I have decided to write a narrative to tell the story of Jake and my trip to Iraq. I was the only parent to enter a war zone to go to where their child was killed.

On April 1, 2003, Jake gave his life for the freedom of this great country and for the freedom of every American.

On this day, Jake and his platoon where given orders to recon the Pipeline Bridge located in south As Samawah. As the platoon went through the guard post, they were not told that this area was under heavy fire from the enemy.

As the platoon traveled, they noticed that the area was quiet, which gave them an eerie feeling. They also noticed a lot of shell casings on the ground. As the platoon pulled into formation, one of the gunner's noticed a man in the bed of a truck with a rocket-propelled grenade aimed at him. He radioed for permission to fire but was told to stand down. When asked again, the rocket-propelled grenade struck his Humvee. Jake saw what was happening and ordered his men to "get the f*** out of there!" As the driver turned around to block Sergeant V.'s Humvee, Jake's Humvee took fourteen gunshots to the passenger side. Jake was able to get off about fifteen rounds before he was shot in the head. While this was happening, Sergeant C. ran from the location of his Humvee and through the line of fire to help the gunner who was hit by the rocket-propelled grenade.

After the gunfight that lasted about two minutes, Jake's Humvee headed back south. As they headed out, they continued to take fire from the enemy.

Jake's gunner was shot three times in the legs. As he was shot, he still kept fighting with the enemy. When the platoon returned to the aid station, the colonel began yelling at the platoon and wanted to know what was going on and who ordered the mission. Later, Cindy and I would find out that the orders came from a lieutenant.

One of Jake's friends tried to save him, but he didn't realize that he had already passed. They laid his body in the back of the aid station. A picture of his mom and me was laid on his body. His body was not moved until the next day.

One of the things that has eaten at me since this day was the colonel who ordered the mission told us that "Jake got what he asked for."

Cindy and I asked for a casualty report after his death. We were told it would come within a couple of weeks. Unfortunately, it never came. We asked again and were told that during the time of war, the army does not have to give a casualty report. I thought it didn't matter during peace or war. The military uses these files to understand where they made mistakes. As a kid growing up, I thought all military were men of honor. I found out over the years that this is not the case. Some would rather be more political than honorable men.

As for the men on that day that were with Jake, they thought Sergeant Corkrean and Sergeant Butler should receive the Medal of Honor for their unselfish actions that day. Enfield and Hale should also receive Silver Stars for their actions. Osgood should receive a Bronze Star for his actions.

I have been in contact with several high-profile people. Mrs. Palin was eager to read my story. Unfortunately, she never called or responded to me. The governor of Kansas and a senator also offered assistance, but they ignored my many attempts to contact their office.

As I close this chapter in my life, I hope Jake would approve of what I found out about April 1, 2003. I know upper ranking officers will never tell the whole truth, but

I know most of what happened. With the help of God, I can live with that. I do wonder what Jake would be like today. I wonder if he would be married and have a family. I wonder if he would still be in the service. I wonder what he would say after all that has happened in the last ten years. May God forgive those that don't step forward for a fallen soldier. I will never forget, but I do forgive all.

# A Valediction

Below is a poem that was written by Sara Elmer for Jacob Butler when he deployed for his first tour to Kuwait. They were close, but both decided to hold off on a relationship until he was out of the military. That opportunity never came. She read it at his funeral service, adding that he touched many lives, loved life, and took every opportunity to make the most of it. May he always live on in our memories and never be forgotten.

I see you fade into the distance,
And know that I'll miss you more every instant.
Even though you may be far away,
There's nothing you can do or say,
To make me not love you.
I already miss your love and affection,
I couldn't have made a better selection.

I will love you till the end of time,
Knowing that, in my heart, you'll always be mine.
In these tough times it's good to know,
Who stands beside you when you're feeling low.
Even though you may be far away,
There's nothing you can do or say,
To make me not love you.

# Biography

Jim Butler was born on April 24, 1956, in Kansas City, Missouri. He lived on a farm just outside of Shawnee, Kansas, then moved into the city limits. At that time, Shawnee was a small town with nothing but gravel roads and stop signs.

He married Cindy Aune on April 19, 1975. They had five boys: James, Josh, Joe, Jake, and Justin. Joe and Jake were twins. He has worked in carpentry his whole life.

After they were married and had kids, they moved to Merriam, Kansas, where they lived until 1990. They decided to move and ended up in Wellsville, Kansas. They are still living there to this day, and Jim is still working in carpentry. He is still married to Cindy, the same beautiful and loving woman.

# Photographs

Pic 1: Jacob Lee Butler

Pic 2: The night before Jake left. His nephew, Jess, Grandpa, Grandma and Niece KK

Pic 3: Jake's head stone

Pic 4: The night before Jake left, his nephew, Jess, is playing with his Army gear

Pic 5: As Samawah, Iraq. The hole in the ground used to have a fence surrounding it. This is where the Iraqi soldiers were hiding before ambushing Jake's platoon.

Pic 6: Jake and his brother, Justin, in their new go-carts

Pic 7: Jake's funeral service

Pic 8: Ceremony for the Purple Heart and Gold Star

Pic 9: Jake's brothers: Justin, Joe, Josh and James; his parents: Jim and Cindy; and his grandparents: Nancy and Robert

Pic 10: The family at Disney World, 1990

Pic 11: One of Jake's first bottle-fed calves, Bobbit.

Pic 12: Jake loved fishing. Pictured here with a friend.

Pic 13: The family in front of Butler's Bait and Tackle.

Pic 14: From the left: Josh, Justin, James, Joe and Jake

Pic 15: The accident in my dream. Everyone survived.

Pic 16: Jake's 1986 Trans Am

Pic 17: Jake training in the Mojave Desert in January 2003
Pic 18: Jake and his twin brother, Joe, before Jake left for Iraq

Pic 19: Jake's dad, Jim, and his mother, Cindy, on President's Day weekend in 2003

Pic 20: Jake's first tour to Kuwait, Halloween 1998

Pic 21: Jake sitting on the hood of his Humvee in Kuwait City

Pic 22: Jake and his twin brother, Joe, walking on the beach in Texas

Pic 23: Jake takes down the yellow ribbon when he returned from Kuwait in 1998.

Pic 24: The "Pipeline" bridge in Iraq.

Pic 25: Jake's last truck, kept by his parents, and decorated for a troop
rally

Pic 26: Silver Star ceremony awarding SGT Jacob Lee Butler

Pic 27: Jim Butler speaking at a troop rally in 2003

Pic 28: The "Pipeline" bridge intersection, where Jake's platoon took heavy gunfire

Pic 29: Jake's unit, friends and family gather at his home after they returned from Iraq

Pic 30: Jim and Joe Butler saying goodbye at the airport before Jim departed for Iraq to honor his son, Jake.

Pic 31: Jake's unit, friends and family gather at his grave site to say goodbye after they returned from Iraq